The School Board Effect

The School Board Effect

Impact of Governing Style on Student Achievement

Alexander U. Ikejiaku, Ph.D.

AuthorHouse™ LLC
1663 Liberty Drive
Bloomington, IN 47403
www.authorhouse.com
Phone: 1-800-839-8640

Published by AuthorHouse 10/31/2013

ISBN: 978-1-4918-0183-3 (sc)
ISBN: 978-1-4918-0184-0 (hc)
ISBN: 978-1-4918-0185-7 (e)

Library of Congress Control Number: 2013913753

This book is printed on acid-free paper.

For presentations and speaking engagements,
log on to: www.schoolboardleadership.com

Table of Contents

PART ONE

PART TWO

PART THREE

PART FOUR

Preface

School boards adopt certain governing styles once they are constituted based on dominant characteristics and predispositions of their members. And, the style a school board ultimately adopts can be good or bad, helpful or hurtful to the school district's educational program. A governing style that is supportive and stabilizing to a school district's administration creates conditions for improved student achievement, while a governing style that is non-supportive or disruptive impacts student achievement negatively.

The idea for this book came from a doctoral dissertation I wrote in 2000 as a graduate student at the State University of New York at Buffalo. When I made the decision to conduct the doctoral research, I was merely exercising intellectual curiosity under the general topic of school board governance and leadership. Little did I know that I would end up working for two school districts in two states—New York and Illinois—in capacities that made it possible for me to work closely with school boards. My subsequent interactions with them would often remind me of certain chapters, or passages, or even whole sections of the dissertation. In other words, there would be constant "aha moments" when I would say to myself, "Aha . . . I wrote about that in my dissertation!"

My early sense of the amount of public interest in my dissertation topic became evident even while the study was being conducted. A total of 128, or 80.5%, of the respondents actually asked to receive copies of the study findings upon its completion. This number is unusually high but not altogether surprising given that the subject matter is of great interest and curiosity to school board members, superintendents, parents, and the community at large.

Furthermore, during the intervening years since I completed my doctoral studies and the dissertation, some graduate students from various universities have contacted me to inquire about it. I was also contacted by one of my best friends, Tobias Ekeze, who let me know that I motivated him to pursue—and ultimately earn—a doctorate in education as well. He also informed me that my dissertation was one of the required readings in one of his graduate level Methods courses at the University of Buffalo. That was a piece of gratifying and welcome news!

While combing through the education literature recently, I came across a piece of research by the Institute for Policy and Economic Development at the University of Texas at El Paso, Texas, which referenced/cited my dissertation in its own study of school board governing styles. These contacts and references, singly or in combination, made me believe that what began as intellectual curiosity in a doctoral program had become real and concrete for me down the road and was, therefore, worthy of being transformed into a book.

Finally, while I was serving as director of human resources for the Springfield Public Schools, I functioned as the chief advisor to the superintendent on all personnel matters, including general administration, recruitment, selection and hiring, collective bargaining, and several other high-level functions in human capital management. The role invariably brought me face-to-face with board members, individually or in groups, at executive sessions as well as during public meetings. And, with the knowledge I already acquired about school boards and their policy-making style, everything the board did took on an important meaning for me. In fact, the interaction among board members or between the board and the superintendent was often seen by me through a special lens: seeing evidence of the board's policy-making style and making the connection to how those interactions impact district governance and, ultimately, student achievement.

Dedication

I dedicated the dissertation to my wife, Peace, and my children Amanda, Victor, Chiamaka, and Austin for all that they missed or endured while I was pursuing the doctoral program. I am now including the following individuals in the book dedication: My last child, Chidera Destiny Ikejiaku, who was not yet born when I completed my dissertation; my father, Chief Alexander E. Ikejiaku, Sr.; and my mother, Mrs. Cecilia Ikejiaku, who left this world on August 9, 2009. And, for a very special and personal reason, I also dedicate this book to the Nwanne Di Na Mba Association of Central Illinois under the able leadership of Mr. Robert Onyewuchi.

Acknowledgements

The acknowledgements in the dissertation version of this book are still worthy, so I will repeat them here. This book would never have materialized without the love and support of my family, the guidance of my dissertation committee, and the general support of my friends and coworkers. Specifically, I want to acknowledge:

- My wife, Peace, who took on the role of mother and father for our children during my long absences from home. I also thank my children: Amanda, Victor, Angelica, Austin and my last child, Chidera, for their love and understanding in my career.

- My mother, Mrs. Cecilia Ikejiaku, who passed away on August 9, 2009, but who worried so much about me while I was in school and prayed constantly for my success. I also acknowledge my father, Chief Alexander E. Ikejiaku, who remained in Nigeria to stabilize the "home" branch of the Ikejiaku family.

- My father-in-law, Chief Richard Nwokocha, who believed in me and encouraged me to soar as high as my dreams would take me; may his soul rest in peace. Not to be left out is my mother-in-law, Mrs. Rhoda C. Nwokocha, who is a deeply religious person who helped to sustain the two families with prayer.

- Professor James Conway, who taught the section of the dissertation course I took while I was in the doctoral program. It was actually Professor Conway who gave me a copy of the journal article on school boards that gave rise to the dissertation project.

- Members of my dissertation committee: Dr. Lynn Ilon (chairperson), Dr. Stephen Jacobson, and Dr. Lauri Johnson for their diligent guidance of the dissertation.

- My friends and well-wishers who constantly cheered me on and helped me to maintain focus: the Honorable Gladys Santiago, Sir Larry Allen, who I call my "colleague extraordinaire," Ms. Marie Sidoti, and others.

- My employer during the time I was in graduate school, the Rochester City Council, for supporting my efforts. Specifically, I thank the Honorable Lois J. Geiss (council president at the time) and my immediate supervisor at the time, William F. Sullivan (chief legislative assistant), for being flexible with my work schedule at certain points during my educational program. I also thank all my coworkers for their general support and for picking up whatever extra work would have been occasioned by my planned absences from the office.

- My former colleagues and close friends at the Rochester City School District (Rochester, New York), Dr. Edward Yansen, Mike Sausa, Audrey Cummings, and Sheryl Scotto, who have been supportive of me and my family all these years.

- The husband and wife team of Jim and Patricia Speers, who wholeheartedly welcomed me into their home during my early years in the United States and helped me to lay the foundation for a hopeful future.

- Dr. Kierian K. C. Nwugwo, who provided guidance to me when I was planning to come to the United States for the first time, and who welcomed me into his home for a long while until I grew my own wings.

PART ONE

CHAPTER I

Introduction

Every school board has a unique governing style

There is ample evidence in the education literature that every school board adopts a certain governing style once it is constituted, and the adopted style invariably affects the internal dynamics of district administration. This means that whichever governing style a board adopts is likely to impact district administration and ultimately have a *domino effect* on student achievement. This book explores the link between school board *governing style* and *district governance* and how such dynamic interplay ultimately impacts *student achievement.*

The ongoing quest for what ails public education

Everywhere we look these days, the wave of national education reform that began some 30 years ago with the *Nation at Risk Report* is still alive and well today and appears to be gaining additional momentum (National Commission on Excellence in Education Report, 1983). This means that there is a desperate and continuing search for "what ails public education." This search has no doubt given rise to several national pieces of legislative actions and mandates, including the recent landmark *amendment* and reauthorization of the Elementary and Secondary Education Act (ESEA), known as the No Child Left Behind legislation (2002); the federal Race to the Top legislation (2010); and Common Core State Standards (2010), to name a few. There have also been quite a few state-level legislative actions on education reform in states such as Wisconsin, New York, and Illinois, where key pieces of legislative reforms have been passed on issues such as teachers' right to organize, tenure, and performance evaluation.

In the November 2011 issue of the American School Board Journal, Rader and McCarthy wrote about a recent wave of school governance councils that are being created through legislative initiatives in a number of states throughout the United States as part of the effort to "improve public education." Among the states that are experimenting with governance councils are Connecticut, California, Kentucky, and Illinois. These governance councils are supposed to play an important advisory role in how schools are run, analyzed, and resourced in the hope that doing so will engender strong community participation and accountability.

Every reform effort presupposes that something or a combination of things is *causing* the problem. The list of what is believed to be wrong with public education is usually long, depending on who is surveyed. Here are some of the most frequently mentioned variables:

1. Teacher quality
2. Class size
3. Lack of adequate funding
4. Teacher pay
5. Non-rigorous standards
6. Poor principal leadership
7. Tenure and union influence

8. Absence of national standards
9. Socioeconomic status of students

The one variable that is often left off the list is *school board governing style.* This variable seldom appears on the list of what ails public education despite the fact that it has been discussed extensively in the literature as being a critical factor in our education system. This is a major omission! ***This book, therefore, adds school board governing style to the list and pushes for practical fixes to how boards ought to govern in order to improve educational outcomes.***

The role of school boards is often ill defined and poorly understood

In addition to the fact that school board governance seldom makes the list of what ails public education, the role of school boards is said to be ill defined and poorly understood. Of particular interest, and germane to this discussion, are two major aspects of educational governance: the ***policy-making role*** of the board and the ***district administration role*** of the superintendent. These have traditionally and necessarily been viewed as being sequential in nature and functionally separate (Anderson 1992, Greene 1990, 1992; Luehe 1989; Relic, 1986).

But in many instances, particularly in larger heterogeneous districts (Institute for Educational Leadership [IEL], 1986), there are no clear demarcations between where the role of policy-making ends and administration begins (Tallerico, 1989). In fact, in the education literature, these two areas tend to be broadly or ill defined; they are potentially contradictory and confusing to the reader (New York State Education Law, pp. 233-295). For example, the language in the New York State Education Law is so ambiguous that it tends to give the board and the superintendent room to interpret or define their rights, roles, and responsibilities liberally. The effect of this type of a situation is that the board and the superintendent often find themselves squaring off in a power struggle.

The absence of clear role demarcations, therefore, makes it almost inevitable that different boards will adopt different policy-making styles, shaped to some degree by their environment and their collective educational philosophy. The education literature contains information on a variety of decision-making styles by school boards that would seem to confirm a "different-strokes-for-different-folks" approach to school district governance (Blanchard, 1975; Greene, 1992; Katz, 1993; Lutz & Gresson, 1980; Tallerico, 1989; Thurlow Brenner, Sullivan, & Dalton. 2002).

The question of why boards operate with so many different styles when the nation's public educational objective is the same remains a curious one (Lutz, 1980; Natale, 1990, p. 17; Weil, 1989, New York State Education Department [NYSED], 1998). It is, however, one that can be understood in the context of business and management, where the *virtues of effective management* are constantly extolled. Just as management theorists espouse the view that workers have different levels of motivations and therefore require different types of management and supervision (Bolman & Deal, 1991, pp. 125-131), the mere existence of different types of board policy-making styles can be viewed in the same light. Given that each school district is different—in terms of who the board members are, what their beliefs and educational philosophies are, who the superintendent is, and what his or her beliefs are, as well as the overall social and political culture—each situation is likely to call for different approaches to educational governance.

Other critical variables in the *district governance* milieu

It should be pointed out that any effort to gauge the potential impact of a board's style on performance needs to be balanced by the recognition that there are other mitigating factors at work as well. These include, but are not limited to, the superintendent's personality and leadership skills, the social and cultural climate in the district, and the level of personal and professional commitment of the school administrators and teachers.

Katz (1993), for instance, suggested in a theoretical piece that the administrative style of the superintendent is an important element in board-superintendent relations, not just the policy-making style of the board. He claims that the extent to which board styles are adequately "matched-up" with those of the superintendent, the board-superintendent relationship will either be "successful" or "unsuccessful." Katz's (1993) premise definitely resonates in real life relative to the challenges of board-superintendent relationships.

Also, in a classic piece on how to manage schools more effectively, Karl Weick (1982) makes the point that certain mitigating factors can get in the way of achieving intended results in school settings. He described schools as loosely coupled systems that do not lend themselves easily to conventional management theory. This would mean that an intended policy developed at the top of the leadership pyramid might end up not being implemented in accordance with its true objective or fidelity. Therefore, even though the board members are believed to be the body that formulates district policy, their influence on educational outcomes can be attenuated by other factors during the implementation process.

The governing style of school boards really matters

The policy-making style of school boards matters a great deal because each school board governs in different and unique ways: some govern very well, others do not govern very well, and some are somewhere in the middle.

Policies devised by school boards affect the lives of millions of children and their parents in this country. There seems to be little dispute over the fact that a school board's policy-making style can affect the substance of the actual policies. Such variations in style can be potentially beneficial to the educational system, especially since it would seem to offer boards the opportunity to be creative in running their respective districts. In the context of education, however, those stylistic variations or "creative" ways of running the district must ultimately serve the needs of students.

In reality, not all school board actions and decision-making styles advance the goal of education, especially if they occur in different forms and impact aspects of district governance differently (Greene, 1992). For instance, an issue in one district can elicit different responses in another district depending on the environment and the policy-making style of the board. Therefore, the extent to which educational research is able to identify "functional" and "dysfunctional" policy-making styles will help the system to fulfill its primary objective of serving the needs of the learner. If it can be demonstrated that district administration is impacted differently by various policy-making styles, then the questions that must be asked are: ***Can specific policy-making styles be associated with either good or poor educational outcomes? If so, what are the dynamics at work in the various styles that would yield such differential outcomes?***

Why and how this study was conducted

The purpose of the doctoral study was twofold: First, to determine the policy-making style of school boards and separate them into two groups using Greene's (1992) "*professional-political*" classification model; second, compare the student achievement indicators of the two groups to see if there are statistically significant differences between them that might be associated with the policy-making styles of their boards. The study was built upon Kenneth Greene's (1992) "Models of School Board Policy-Making," in which he found that boards differ in their role—and subsequent impact—on certain aspects of school district administration, especially with regard to district personnel. Their policy-making styles tend to be associated with how they function or operate in this crucial policy-making role.

My own doctoral study on this topic, therefore, amounted to an extension of Greene's (1992) inquiry to see whether the observed differential impact of board policy-making styles on governance has a corresponding differential impact on student achievement, or whether such effect is mitigated by other extraneous factors. If the former turns out to be the case, then it would mean that the action of school boards at the governance level sets off a chain of events that ultimately affects the educational outcomes in their districts.

Finally, this study was designed to serve one additional accessory purpose: to determine whether a community's socioeconomic status predisposes its school to adopting a certain governing style. If so, this would imply a subsequent role for "poverty" or "affluence" in determining the educational outcomes in the district. It is important to point out that the treatment of socioeconomic status (SES) here is different from the larger—and debatable—question of whether SES directly affects educational achievement.

The significance and practical application of the study in the field of education and in the society at large

Education policy stands to benefit from this discussion, especially given that the results of the study revealed at least one pattern of performance gains by one type of governing style over the other. These stylistic variations can, therefore, be helpful or harmful depending on how they affect the ability of the districts to fulfill their basic educational objective: serve the needs of the learners (Lutz, 1980; Natale, 1990, p. 17; Weil, 1989). Specifically, the study can be used as follows:

1. As a guide to selecting the type of policy-making style that would work well for each district type; knowing which of the two styles yields higher or lower performance outcomes becomes both important and instructive. Based on such

information, educational policy makers can retool the system in a way that would promote or maximize the style that works and de-emphasize that which does not work.

2. To help with the decision to invest money in the training or other resources for board members in order to steer them to the desired style. In fact, the importance of training for board members is one that is constantly underscored, as well as advocated for, by school board observers as a way to improve overall board service (Anderson, 1992, p. 15, 17; Banach, 1989, p. 23; Bryant & Grady, 1990, p. 21; Carpenter, 1989, p. 24; Grady & Bryant, 1991; Luehe, 1989). The New York State School Boards Association (NYSSBA), for instance, provides training opportunities for new board members on an ongoing basis and runs ongoing board development sessions for current members in a number of areas, including education law and district management (NYSSBA, 1998).

3. To spur needed debate and reworking of the language of education laws pertaining to district governance in individual states. It is the vagueness and lack of clarity on the law books that are partly responsible for the confusion on board-superintendent roles. A uniform and clearly defined set of roles and expectations for the school board and the superintendent might help to reduce conflict and turf wars between the two key players in the district.

Organization of this book

The chapters in this book are organized under four main parts and eighteen chapters as follows:

Part One (chapters I-XI) contains introductory and other information about school board governing styles derived from both the research effort and a review of the education literature. This part also contains the training and professional development module for current or aspiring school board members. Specifically, chapter I is the introduction, which provides the background on school boards and policy-making styles. It also defines the problem under investigation as well as articulates the purpose of the study. The significance of the study identifies some of the potential contributions of the study to the field of education.

Chapters II through VI contain a presentation of the literature review, beginning with an introduction of the reader to school boards, followed by a discussion of some of the decision-making styles of school boards. The chapters also discuss the impact of board styles on school district governance and the potential impact of board orientation on student achievement.

Chapters VII and VIII contain an analysis of the study and a set of recommendations for the reader.

Chapter IX is the outline for the training and professional development module for readers or for current and aspiring board members.

Chapter X contains other noteworthy pieces of information from the original dissertation deemed relevant for inclusion in the book.

Finally, chapter XI contains the author's ten important *takeaways* for the reader. This is a *must-read* for all education stakeholders!

Part Two (chapters XII and XIII) contains more detailed and technical information on the *methodology, results, and findings* of the research study. Specifically, chapter XII is a presentation of the methodology that describes how the study was conducted. It identifies the respondents in the study and describes the survey instruments and how they were used to categorize school boards according to their policy-making styles. It also describes the types of statistical analyses that were used in the study to test for differences in the student achievement indicators of the two groups. Chapter XIII is a presentation of the results and findings, including the results of the statistical analyses that were conducted in the following order: (1) statewide sample, (2) urban, (3) suburban, and (4) rural.

Part Three (chapter XIV-XVIII) contains accessory materials that touch on certain study considerations employed by the author. Some of the key terms and concepts that are referenced in the study are also defined to facilitate reading and comprehension of the subject matter. Specifically, this group of chapters provides the opportunity to reflect on the data and the findings, a discussion of the limitations of the study, and integration of the various perspectives so that conclusions can, in turn, be drawn from them. This part also contains a chapter on the original set of recommendations that was in the dissertation. It concludes with a review of the student achievement indicators and New York State's education law on board-superintendent roles.

Part Four contains the references cited in the study and end notes for the reader's convenience.

CHAPTER II

What the Education Literature Says About School Boards

This literature review begins with a general background on school boards and their leadership roles and expectations in district management. It then goes on to discuss some of the key studies on school board policy-making styles and their impact on district administration and, ultimately, student performance. Also, a review of the selected educational achievement measures is presented as a way of exploring possible associations between policy-making styles and performance outcomes.

The school board form of district governance

School boards are governmental bodies that derive their authority from, and act on behalf of, state governments to oversee the formulation of educational policies in local school districts (IEL, 1986; Lutz, 1980; R. Heller, personal communication, November 1996; Simon, 1986). Their existence amounts to a convenient arrangement by state governments to delegate the power to oversee schools to local entities that are familiar with, and responsive to, the local scene. This system of district management has been around for over 300 years (IEL, 1980; Lutz, 1980).

Board members come into board service either through appointment by the chief executive officer of the municipality or through an election process. As of the late 1990s and early 2000s when the study was conducted, there were approximately 97,000 school board members in the nation serving on some 15,000 local school boards (Lutz, 1980; Lutz & Gresson, 1980; Weil, 1989). The profile of a board member at that time was a 41– to 50-year-old White male, who is married with at least one child, and who has an average board experience of 1-5 years. He would typically be a homeowner in the district and is often a holder of some type of an advanced degree and has a job in a professional or managerial field earning between $40,000 and $49,000 per year (Lutz, 1980). [Note: the $40,000+ earnings figure for a typical board member at that time has more than doubled in the intervening years since Lutz's profile was developed.] A typical school board has seven members who come into service mainly through community democratic elections (Lutz, 1980; Seaton, Underwood, & Fortune, 1992).

Individual board members or an entire school board can be preempted or removed from office through one of three ways: (1) if members are serving by virtue of having been appointed to the board, the appointing officer can either rescind the appointment or refuse to renew the term of office upon its expiration; (2) if they are serving as a result of having been elected, they will stop serving if they lose an election or decline to run for reelection; but, (3) regardless of whether a board is appointed or elected, the state commissioner for education, who is fully empowered by law to oversee education, has the power to remove individual board members or an entire school board by showing cause. However, this kind of harsh takeover or removal action is usually a tool of last resort (Ritter, 1997).

Conflicts between school boards and superintendents

There are inherent contradictions in the public expectations and role of school board members (Greene, 1990, p. 363; 1992, p. 220). Three such contradictions are as follows:

1. They are expected to provide "lay control" over the complex business of running the district (IEL, 1986).
2. They are also expected to be sophisticated enough to deal with the tough educational issues in the district and to be knowledgeable enough to hold the superintendent accountable.
3. They are sometimes given the impression that they are political representatives who must adopt an advocacy stance in representing their constituencies, when, in fact, they really should not operate that way. Greene (1990), for instance, noted that in some situations, parents and community groups "view board members as representatives who should respond to their demands" (p. 363). With all these conflicting expectations, board members' behaviors often become inconsistent.

It is, therefore, the cumulative effect of all these conflicting expectations, coupled with the ill-defined nature of the job (Tallerico, 1989), that causes school board members all over the country to adopt what Zeigler (1975) called schizophrenic personalities, implying that their behavior tends to be all over the map. This, in turn, means that battles are constantly being waged over power encroachments, with superintendents accusing boards of meddling with district administration and boards accusing superintendents of usurping their policy-making powers (Hentges, 1986; Relic, 1986; Smith, 1986; Trotter & Downey, 1989, p. 21). In reality, each side is generally right in their respective accusation of the other because the demarcation between their roles and responsibilities is fuzzy at best. Therefore, the absence of a common understanding or agreement between the board and superintendent as to each other's roles would remain a major source of conflict and friction in board-superintendent relations.

Clarifying the role of school boards

The school board literature contains some clear and unequivocal declarations and clarifications of what the role of school board members should be:

- They are supposed to function as trustees of education, with no allegiance whatsoever to those who appoint or elect them (Banach, 1989; Carpenter, 1989, p. 24; IEL, 1986).

- They have an obligation to ensure that the educational environment in their districts adequately "serves the needs of learners" (Lutz, 1980; Natale, 1990, p. 17; Weil, 1989). Given their lay backgrounds, they are supposed to defer to the expertise of the superintendent on administrative and educational matters (Anderson 1992, p. 17; Greene 1990, 1992; Luehe 1989; Relic, 1986).

- They are to avoid partisan politics and not become involved in the day-to-day administration of school districts (Bryant & Grady,

1990, p. 21; Greene, 1990, p. 363; Relic, 1986; Smith, 1986; Tucker & Zeigler, 1980, p.142;).

- They are not to run the schools, but rather to set educational policy and ensure that the schools are well run by the superintendent (Anderson, 1992; Greene, 1992; Luehe, 1989; Simon, 1986, p. 8; Weil, 1989).

So, it can be surmised from the declarations and clarifications above that the roles for the board and superintendent should be different—with ***the board playing the role of policy maker*** and ***the superintendent playing the role of implementer.***

CHAPTER III

The Wide Continuum of School Board Governing Styles

The school board literature contains several policy-making models that have been proposed by various researchers—a recognition that school boards go about their policy-making role in a variety of ways. In developing their models, the researchers consider the dominant characteristics of school boards, their expressed or implied educational philosophy, their operating environment, and their behavior toward the superintendent and the public. These provide the basis for categorizing boards into one style or the other.

Another research convention gleaned from the literature is a tendency by researchers to categorize school board policy-making styles along a style continuum, with most school boards clustering at both ends of the continuum. On one end of this continuum there are boards that are less conflictual, less confrontational, nonpartisan, less responsive to their constituency, and do not meddle in district administration. And on the other end of the continuum there are those that are conflictual, confrontational, overly responsive to special interests and other constituencies, and meddlesome in district administration operations. School boards, therefore, can fall anywhere on this continuum, although evidence in the literature suggests that they tend to cluster at both ends of the style continuum (Greene, 1992, p. 225).

Figure 1

Policy-making continuum (Greene, 1992)

Professional	**Political**
Nonpartisan	Highly partisan
Less conflictual	Highly conflictual
Less confrontational	Highly confrontational
Less responsive to constituents	Overly responsive to constituents
Less meddling with administration	Overly meddlesome with administration

Using such broad distinctions, researchers, in turn, attach semantic labels that support their basic premise, as was the case in Blanchard's (1975) unipolar versus bipolar style; Lutz and Gresson's (1980) elite versus arena style; Tallerico's (1989) passive-acquiescent versus restive-vigilant style; Greene's (1992) professional versus political style; and Katz's (1993) corporate versus familial style. A review of the work by each of the aforementioned researchers follows.

Unipolar, bipolar, and nonpolar policy-making styles

An interdisciplinary study by Blanchard (1975) was among the earlier attempts to study school board policy-making styles and behaviors using concepts and techniques from small group research. In the study, Blanchard analyzed the decisional practices and styles of school boards by examining the effects of "conflict" and "cohesion" variables on decision making. In other words, the decision style of the boards was classified based on the degree of conflict or cohesion that exists in the group: the terms "bipolar" and "unipolar" describe each group's dynamics. The bipolar classification refers to boards that experience substantial conflict and form identifiable blocs or cliques that clash with each other. In the unipolar classification, there is less conflict and little or no identifiable blocs. The "nonpolar" category is somewhere in the middle and is said to experience conflict "without discernible patterns or consistent blocs" (p. 236).

Blanchard (1975) surveyed 528 of the 960 school board members in Kentucky to determine the presence or absence, as well as the degree, of conflict that exists within the various school boards. School districts were included in the analysis only if there were at least five or more respondents from their district; this was done to ensure that the opinions of the respondents would be representative of the entire board. The questionnaire also sought to determine the presence or absence of voting blocs as a way of getting at the degree of open-mindedness among board members. Voting behavior, in terms of whether they are unanimous or nonunanimous, was used to operationalize intra-board conflict, while open-mindedness was measured by members' perception of the existence of identifiable blocs within the board.

There was a 55% percent return rate, resulting in the inclusion of 528 school districts in the study pool. In the end, the study turned out to confirm the researcher's prediction. In accordance with the descriptions of the various board styles, it was found that bipolar boards tend to exhibit greater conflict (more nonunanimous voting behavior with identifiable blocs) than the unipolar boards that have the least amount of conflict (more unanimous voting behavior with little or no identifiable blocs). The nonpolar category, which is a neutral category, exhibited moderate conflict with a mixture of unanimous and nonunanimous voting behavior, and without any discernible or consistent blocs.

This study is relevant because it is another example of documented evidence of the existence of differences in school board policy-making styles and how they might impact the management of school districts. The study is limited to some extent by the fact that it was conducted only in one state, potentially limiting its generalizability outside the state. The author also recognizes the need to refine the methodology and to minimize possible subjectivity in the classification of the policy-making styles.

"Elite" and "arena" policy-making styles

Lutz and Gresson (1980) used a political-anthropological approach to examine the policy-making behaviors of school boards, drawing upon existing studies of local political councils. The school boards included in the study were characterized as either "elite" or "arena" based on how the members viewed their role in education. For instance, elite boards view their role as guardians or trustees of the educational system. They also consider themselves to be "a ruling oligarchy" that is removed from, and aloof to, the general public; they govern only in special areas of district governance. The arena boards, on the other hand, see themselves as representatives or delegates of certain factions of the community. They also tend to represent a strong community life and govern more broadly. It should be noted that the choice of the word "arena" was a deliberate one, as it describes policy-making sessions as the arena in which representatives of various community interests come together to battle issues out with one another.

This was a qualitative study in which several ethnographic techniques were utilized, including nonparticipant observation, interviews, and document analysis. Two nine-member school boards in Pennsylvania were selected for the study based on how well they fit the profile of the two kinds of boards that Lutz and Gresson (1980) described above: i.e., whether they are conflict-free and operate on the basis of broad consensus or have a high degree of conflict and low consensus with split voting behaviors instead.

The researchers found that the two boards held certain fundamentally different views and acted according to the characteristic differences described above. For instance, in District A, which was representative of an elite board, it was reported that the members tended to think of themselves as the guardians of the public. There was also a strong, positive, and trusting board-superintendent relationship, to the point that the superintendent thought of himself as part of the board, and the board treated him as a "non-voting member" of their group (pp. 130-131).

In District B, which is the arena equivalent, a series of conflict situations were noted early in the study, including the following observation by an assistant high school principal: "The board has a past orientation, some present, and little future. They don't like to fight, but lately there has been a lot of five-to-four decisions—you'll have to watch for that. It's revolving around the superintendent, whom they want to get rid of" (Lutz & Gresson, 1980, p.134).

In this district, decisions were made in conflict situations and often nonunanimously. There were also references to constant pleadings and petitioning by citizens and professional groups seeking the reversal of unpopular board decisions. In fact, it was noted that one group attended one of the school board meetings to see about "getting our teacher back" (Lutz & Gresson, 1980, p. 134)—a clear indication that the board gets involved in the personnel matters of the district. Lutz and Gresson (1980) also reported that, "Four months after data collection ended, the board voted to reduce the superintendent's salary ten percent for the following year. This action precipitated the superintendent's resignation, effective at the beginning of the new fiscal year, which was less than two months away" (p.137).

In spite of the age-old criticism that qualitative studies are nonscientific and therefore tend to be subjective in nature, this study adequately contrasts differences in the philosophy and behavior of two different boards in two school districts. The findings show that the two boards differ in their views, as well as their approaches to education, and consequently behaved in ways that had a differential impact on district management.

In District A, where the superintendent and the board had a harmonious relationship, there were very few conflict situations or disruptions in the running of the district. District B, on the other hand, appeared to have all the makings of a chaotic school district, with conflict engulfing not only the board, but also the board and superintendent together; the superintendent was ultimately forced to resign.

Passive-acquiescent, restive-vigilant, and proactive-supportive policy-making styles

In a study of how school boards operate behind the scenes, Tallerico (1989) interviewed 26 school board members and 18 superintendents in a major metropolitan area in the Southwest. Her interview questions sampled the "perceptions and opinions of respondents on how, when, and where the work of local leadership in public education occurs" (p. 26). First, Tallerico examined the responses from the interviews looking for information on unique characteristics that distinguish the boards from one another. She ultimately used this information to classify board members as follows: (1) passive-acquiescent, (2) proactive-supportive, and (3) restive-vigilant.

According to Tallerico (1989), the passive-acquiescent board members are those who rely totally on the superintendent and trust his or her judgment for information and advice. They do not get involved in the school system's activities and are usually conscientious about reading and processing information presented to them by the administrative staff. The restive-vigilant board members, on the other hand, rely less on the superintendent and more on their constituency. They often try to "build support for their objectives and tend to oversee the school system with vigor." They are "not reluctant to monitor or question the superintendent's information and advice, and stand ready to apply a brake to administrative activities" (pp. 26). The proactive-supportive board is in the middle; they are described as being active in school affairs but are generally trusting of the superintendent and his or her staff. They "tend to keep the peace, build support, and keep the lid on controversy" (p. 26).

Like the other studies reviewed above, this one also acknowledges the existence of differences in school board policy-making styles, including descriptions of how each style might impact district governance. Of greater relevance here are the descriptions provided by Tallerico (1989) on how boards of different orientations relate to the superintendent.

Professional and political policy-making styles

In a study of school board styles, Greene (1992) grouped the various board policy-making styles into "professional" and "political" categories based on conceptual distinctions he found in the school board literature. Such distinctions were based on the philosophies and beliefs of school board members as well as on their behavior toward the superintendent. Boards were classified as "professional" if they viewed educational policy-making as "primarily a technical, expertise-based process" that relied heavily on the recommendations of the superintendent. But they were classified as "political" if they viewed the process as one in which the board represents community interests, and they bargained with the superintendent.

In order to classify school boards into the two categories, Greene (1992) surveyed school board presidents from 368

New Jersey school districts to determine (1) the degree of responsiveness of the collective board to parents and community groups, (2) the degree of intra-board conflict as measured by percent of "unanimous decisions," and (3) the degree of reliance on the specialized knowledge and guidance of the superintendent. With the board classification in place, Greene set out to determine what factors dictate board orientation. He tested five variables mentioned in the school board literature as potential factors, including district socioeconomic status, district size, the degree of community conflict, degree of electoral competition, and community dissatisfaction.

To determine the consequences of board orientation on governance, Greene (1992) analyzed the survey responses on the relative responsibility of boards and superintendents in the area of curriculum, personnel, and district finances as well as on how boards perceive their policy leadership and agenda setting in those same areas (Anderson, 1992; Greene, 1992). The thinking behind this approach was that boards operating in a political mode would be more likely to assert their authority and would assume more responsibility for these decisions than would professional boards (Greene, 1992, pp. 230-231); this prediction was later confirmed by the findings.

The study revealed an association between board orientation and school district governance, with a greater tendency for political boards to exercise more responsibility in curriculum, personnel, and district finances. A number of other noteworthy observations were also made in Greene's (1992) study. They include the following: (a) the incidence of professional versus political boards is 61% to 39%, respectively; (b) districts with

1,500 or more students (p. 226) had less community conflict, less electoral competition, and fewer incumbent defeats and were more likely to adopt the professional orientation; and finally, (c) the socioeconomic status of a district did not appear to have any effect on board orientation.

It should be noted that this study represents a major contribution to the field of school board research in the sense that it was a marked departure from the practice of simply classifying the policy-making styles to investigating their impact on governance. And the thinking behind this extra research step by Greene (1992) was valid: fundamental differences in the educational philosophy of school boards underlie their different policy-making styles as well as influence their behavior within the context of district governance. Greene's thinking was validated by his findings, which showed that political boards were more likely than professional boards to get more involved in administrative matters, particularly in the area of personnel management. Specifically, Greene found that political boards

1. tended to exercise more responsibility in curriculum, personnel, and finance areas, with the greatest impact being on personnel issues;

2. were less likely to accept the superintendent's recommendations;

3. tended to (claim responsibility as well as) be responsible for agenda setting; and

4. were less likely to defer to the superintendent and would instead exert more influence on matters of school district governance.

The study is comprehensive in its design in the sense that it provided two broad categories in which the other models can be incorporated. But it had one potential weakness: only one state (New Jersey) was studied, and as such, generalizability of the results to other states might be an issue. But, as he correctly pointed out, conducting the study in a state where the education laws and the electoral system are the same has the advantage of increasing reliability and validity.

Corporate and familial, task-oriented, and relationship-oriented policy-making styles

In an effort to study the policy-making and administrative styles of school boards and superintendents, respectively, Katz (1993) examined (1) the preferred decision-making processes of school boards, that is, whether they prefer written or oral communication; (2) how they perceive their role, i.e., whether there are direct or indirect linkages to staff and to the community; (3) the influence of key board member values on decision making, i.e., whether school mission is tied to student needs or placating the constituency; (4) the attitudes of the board toward their advisement resources, i.e., outside or inside consultants; and (5) preferred superintendent priorities, i.e., whether emphasis is on setting educational objectives or on the craving of visibility in the community.

Based on the outcome of this review, Katz (1993) offered the following distinguishing characteristics of the two kinds of board styles: the "corporate" board is one that "has decision-making processes that are rational, predictable, and data-based; thrives on carefully developed informational reports; has sophisticated understanding of policy and its execution and communicates through the chain of command; prefers goal-setting, long-range planning, and management by objectives as a basis for operations; has a commitment to 'standards' or 'excellence,' rather than loyalty to a community or school system; values expert opinion and outside consultation" (p. 20). Katz further wrote, "Picture in your mind the mythical corporate board meeting in its data-drenched boardroom providing policy and oversight for a large and diverse company" (p. 19). The idea here appears to be that of a professional board that takes its responsibilities seriously, does its homework, and goes about its job in a professional and methodical manner.

"Familial" boards, on the other hand, are those that have "more personalized and affective decision-making processes. They are strongly influenced by personal communication and recent feedback, and are less predictable and less reliant on data; they thrive on informal and oral communication, one-to-one and as a group, (he or she is suspicious of the published report with tables and appendices; this is not a reading board member, but a talking and listening board member); a flexible and situational approach to policy and its execution; the value they place on oral communication obliterates any niceties of chain of command; prefers informal, verbal approaches to planning, and prefers satisfied constituents over measured achievements; is loyal to his community, his school system, rather than to abstractions of standards or excellence; rejects as intrusive any outside or expert opinion and looks inward for resources rather than beyond the school district" (Katz, 1993, p. 20).

Katz (1993) also wrote, "Picture in your mind for the familial board a group of family elders meeting in a church or at the home of one of its leading members, making decisions for a loosely connected clan of cousins, children, and in-laws" (p. 19).

With regard to superintendents, Katz (1993) used the terms "task-oriented" and "relationship-oriented" to describe their style. In the former situation, the superintendent is seen as one who is oriented toward structure, is willing to take primary responsibility for the group, and can be "autocratic, controlling, managing, directive, and task-oriented with his members." Whereas in the latter situation, he shares decision-making and leadership with his group; he can be democratic, permissive, non-directive, considerate of group members' feelings and therapeutic in his leadership" (p. 17).

Katz (1993) suggested that the extent to which board styles are appropriately matched with those of the superintendent, the resulting relationship will either be "successful" or "unsuccessful." He also suggested two potentially successful board-superintendent matchups or combinations as follows: (a) corporate boards with task-oriented superintendents, and (b) familial boards with relationship-oriented superintendents. Simplistic as this may appear, it makes sense that a board that is work oriented and businesslike would work well with a superintendent who is equally businesslike. If a businesslike board is paired with a superintendent who is high on the relationship scale, there is apt to be a *mismatch*, and the two players may have difficulty working with each other.

The true value of Katz's (1993) piece is that although it is completely theoretical, it is informed by extensive literature review and by his professional experience. It adds to—as well as agrees with—other research in suggesting that there is a variety of school board policy-making styles. But, more importantly, the "***match-mismatch***" proposition may in fact be the most critical mitigating factor in the study.

Appearing to support Katz's (1993) match-mismatch position, is a national case study conducted by Steinberger (1994); she profiled four public school districts that were previously in distress, but which gradually bounced back to become successful and exemplary. The districts Steinberger studied were Cherry Creek in Denver, Colorado; Lowpoint-Washburn in northern Illinois; Kenmore-Tonawanda in western New York; and Newport-Mesa in Southern California. Steinberger began her study by surveying the superintendents, board members, and active citizens in each district to gather an historical account of events in the districts. She later examined the data, looking specifically for testimony about the leadership styles and abilities of the superintendents during the transition periods.

The results showed that the superintendents who transformed those districts into success stories appeared to have the right styles, the right vision, or both, which appealed to the board and the community as a whole. They were perceived by many to be competent, open or approachable; they were also seen as possessing good public relations skills. They were, therefore, better able to form their ideas and market them more effectively to the board and to the community than their predecessors. Therefore, to the extent that a superintendent's style matches up well with that of the board, the district will be successful or unsuccessful.

CHAPTER IV

Theoretical Framework: Linking Governing Style, District Administration, and Student Achievement

The theoretical theme in all five studies reviewed above is represented in Figure 2 below. It shows that board policy-making styles (labeled A), influence and are influenced by board beliefs and educational philosophy (labeled B), which in turn influences or dictates how the boards behave (labeled C) within the context of school district governance. This dynamic ultimately impacts educational performance (labeled D). There is also a recognition that a district's academic performance can equally influence the actions of board members (as depicted by the two reverse arrows pointing toward C), causing them to be either more involved or less involved in district administration.

Figure 2

Linking board policy-making styles to student achievement

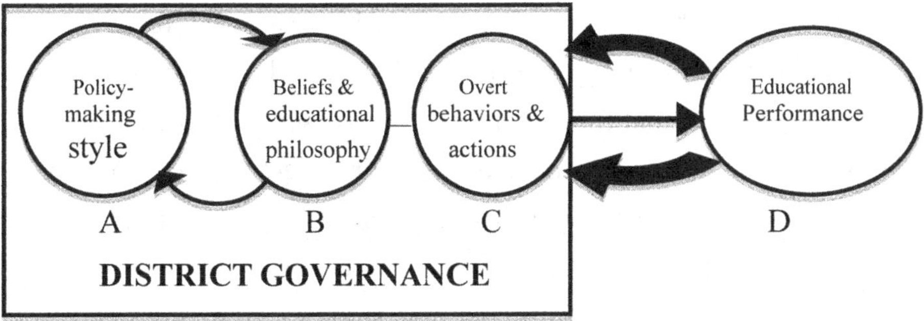

The conceptual framework for this study: The basis for linking board policy-making style to student achievement

The conceptual framework for this study was adapted from Greene (1992), whose work on school board policy-making styles revealed possible connections between board orientation and district governance, with a greater tendency for "political" boards to exercise more responsibility in curriculum, personnel, and district finances. Greene's classification model was adopted in this study for two reasons.

First, it is broad enough to accommodate or account for the two conceptual distinctions in the literature about school board policy-making styles. As shown in Figure 1 above, Greene's "professional" terminology sums up the actions of considerably less aggressive boards on the left side of the continuum, while his "political" terminology describes the more aggressive and meddlesome boards on the right.

Second, Greene's study also represents a major contribution to school board research in the sense that it departed from the routine practice of simply classifying the policy-making styles of school boards and moved toward investigating their impact on governance. Greene (1992) believed, based on his literature review, that fundamental differences in the educational philosophy of school boards underlie their different policy-making styles and might ultimately influence their behavior within the context of district governance. This marked a critical milestone in school board research. In turn, my own study took Greene's work one step further by seeking to determine whether board orientation also impacts student achievement. See Figure 3 for a schematic representation of Greene's model, and the extension of his model by my own (Ikejiaku's) framework.

Figure 3

The theoretical framework—Greene's original model on governance (item 1 through 4) with Ikejiaku's logical extension to student achievement (item 5).

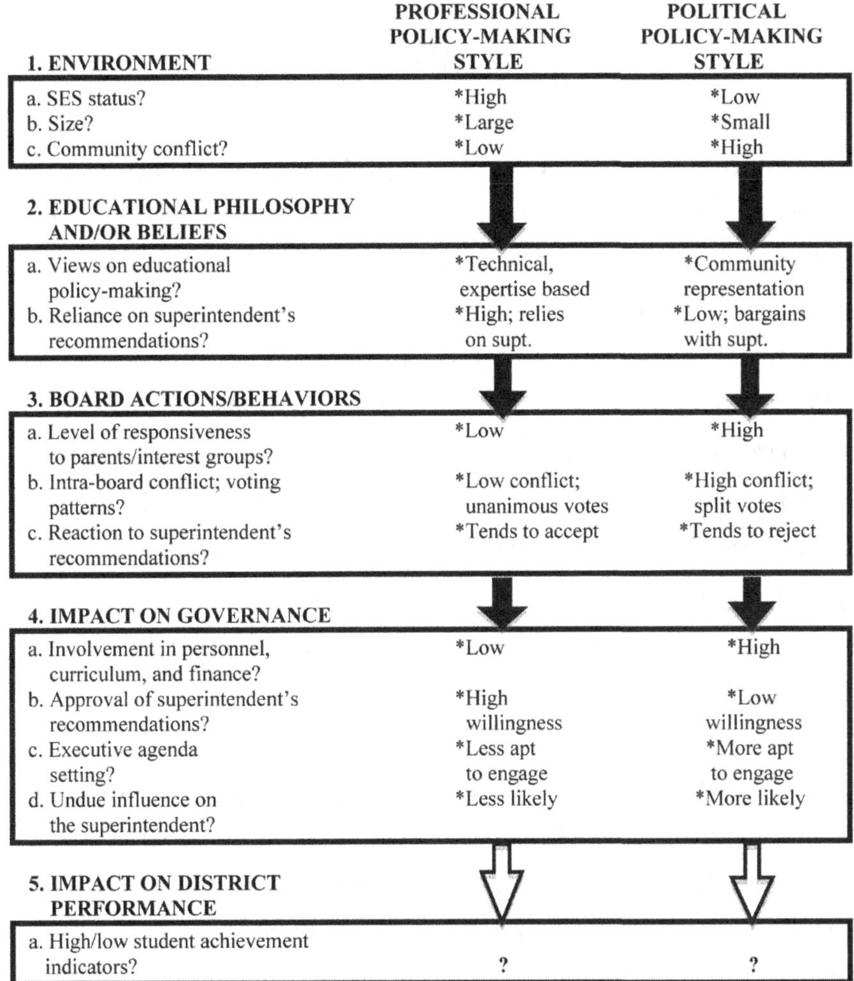

	PROFESSIONAL POLICY-MAKING STYLE	POLITICAL POLICY-MAKING STYLE
1. ENVIRONMENT		
a. SES status?	*High	*Low
b. Size?	*Large	*Small
c. Community conflict?	*Low	*High
2. EDUCATIONAL PHILOSOPHY AND/OR BELIEFS		
a. Views on educational policy-making?	*Technical, expertise based	*Community representation
b. Reliance on superintendent's recommendations?	*High; relies on supt.	*Low; bargains with supt.
3. BOARD ACTIONS/BEHAVIORS		
a. Level of responsiveness to parents/interest groups?	*Low	*High
b. Intra-board conflict; voting patterns?	*Low conflict; unanimous votes	*High conflict; split votes
c. Reaction to superintendent's recommendations?	*Tends to accept	*Tends to reject
4. IMPACT ON GOVERNANCE		
a. Involvement in personnel, curriculum, and finance?	*Low	*High
b. Approval of superintendent's recommendations?	*High willingness	*Low willingness
c. Executive agenda setting?	*Less apt to engage	*More apt to engage
d. Undue influence on the superintendent?	*Less likely	*More likely
5. IMPACT ON DISTRICT PERFORMANCE		
a. High/low student achievement indicators?	?	?

A representation of Greene's (1992) model showing the relationship between board policy-making style and governance. The hollow arrows at the bottom depict the concept and theoretical outflow of this particular study as hypothesized by Ikejiaku (2000).

CHAPTER V

Impact of Governing Style on District Governance

Given that district governance entails a partnership between the board members and the superintendent, many observers agree that it can be—and often is—fraught with peril. It involves the division of critical district management responsibilities between these two educational power elites with different qualifications and different backgrounds (Shannon, 1989, p. 25); it also means that the board-superintendent relationship under these circumstances often becomes inevitably conflictual (IEL, 1986; Smith, 1986, p. 23; Tallerico, 1989). This section of the literature review focuses specifically on the nature and extent of a board's involvement in the management of a school district as determined by its policy-making style or orientation.

Impact on district management and day-to-day administration

In Greene's (1992) study, it was reported that boards that adopt a political policy-making style are more likely to become involved in administrative matters, are less likely to approve changes recommended by the superintendent, and tend to claim responsibility for agenda setting. On the other hand, those that operate in a professional style, are less likely to get involved in administrative matters, more willing to give the superintendent the benefit of the doubt, and tend not to claim responsibility for agenda setting.

Embedded within these observations, is the greater potential for the political style of governing to introduce conflict into the governance milieu, either through increased involvement in administrative matters by not approving changes recommended by the superintendent, or by its tendency to claim responsibility for agenda setting (Allison, 1996; Czarnecki, 1996; Lutz & Gresson, 1980; Spiropulos, 1996; Tallerico, 1989). Such actions amount to crossing the line by the board to meddle with the administrative functions of the superintendent (Bryant & Grady, 1990). And, depending on how these differential propensities or actions are perceived by the superintendent, district management might be impacted in some fashion.

Recall that in the Lutz and Gresson (1980) study on elite-arena boards, there were accounts of districts that have arena boards experiencing ongoing conflicts, as evidenced by "a lot of five-to-four decisions" and the subsequent forced resignation of the superintendent through a deliberate pay cut of an already low salary (p. 134). At a minimum, this and the other recorded actions of the arena board amount to an undue and unwarranted involvement by the board in administrative and personnel matters. This is contrary to elite boards that take a hands-off approach on district administration.

The conceptual distinctions provided by Tallerico (1989) also point to the differential impact of board style on governance. The passive-acquiescent board, for instance, is said to rely heavily on the superintendent for information and direction, it trusts the judgment of the superintendent, and does not become involved in the school system's activities. This is a hands-off approach that would cause less friction and less conflict in district governance. This is unlike the actions of the restive-vigilant group, which run counter to those of its counterpart, and by so doing, engender more intra-board conflict than would normally exist.

There are other ways that a board's policy-making style can impact district governance. For instance, depending on the policy-making style of the board, the educational leadership that is supposed to be provided by the superintendent can either be bolstered or stifled considerably. It is equally plausible that the judgment of the superintendent might become clouded by the realization that he or she is periodically evaluated by the board (Trotter & Downey, 1989) and can be fired by the board (Shannon, 1989, p.26; Tucker & Zeigler, 1980 p. 1). This might, in turn, make the superintendent vulnerable and/or beholden to the politics of the board and the local community (Allison, 1996; Braddom, 1986, p. 28; Lutz & Gresson, 1980; Shannon, 1989, p. 26; Stone, 1988, p. 17; Weller, Brown, & Flynn, 1991).

This means that those boards that respect the dividing line between policy making and district administration would help to bolster or empower the superintendent, while those that do not observe the role differentiation would weaken the superintendency. Therefore, the philosophy, beliefs, styles, or actions of a given school board can impact district governance depending on how much power and control it has or chooses to exercise over the superintendent.

Impact on superintendent turnover—the revolving door syndrome

Other ways that a board's policy-making style can affect the governance of a district is through its indirect effect on superintendent tenure. The national average for superintendent tenure is 6.47 years (Spiropulos, 1996). This means that school districts in which superintendent tenure is substantially below or above this average represent deviations from the norm and therefore deserve special attention. In fact, there is ample evidence in the literature that the board-superintendent relationship is a leading cause of high turnover, both voluntary and involuntary, among superintendents (Allison, 1996; Czarnecki, 1996; Lutz & Gresson, 1980; Spiropulos, 1996). Therefore, depending on how a school board relates to the administrative staff—harmoniously or in a conflictual manner—superintendent tenure might be impacted in some fashion. This, in turn, has the potential to also impact both district governance and the district's overall educational performance.

In the Lutz and Gresson (1980) study, for instance, it was reported that in the arena district, the board caused the superintendent to resign by further cutting his already low salary. At a minimum, this board action probably resulted in: (1) disturbing the smooth operation of the district by disrupting the superintendent's focus; (2) causing the district to face an uncertain future going into the next fiscal year without the leadership of a sitting superintendent; and (3) incurring the expense and delays associated with conducting superintendent searches, which take several months to complete. Additional resources are also likely to be spent on consultants and administrative contracts to keep the district running in the interim. Here, once again, is an example of how operating with the wrong style can disrupt the smooth running of the district.

Consider a story published in the June 15 edition of the *Washington Post* (Baker, 1997, p. A3) in which operatives of the Christian Coalition who serve on the Fort Myers, Florida, school board successfully pushed for the reintroduction of bible history classes in the high schools. This new curriculum was implemented over the objection of the superintendent, who was subsequently fired for "dragging her feet" during the implementation. The district's lawyer who objected to the new curriculum on the grounds that it potentially contravened the United States Constitution was also let go.

Other documented instances of seemingly hostile board action occurred in Kansas and Kentucky as well. In Kansas, for instance, the school board voted to erase "virtually all references to ***evolution*** in a far-reaching victory for creationists" (Rosenberg & Whitmire, 1999). And, in the Kentucky example, the school board voted to put the Ten Commandments on display, potentially in violation of the separation of church and state (Rosenberg & Whitmire, 1999). In these instances, board styles that are rooted in religion impacted the educational program of the districts and, in the Fort Myers situation, also ruined the careers of two seasoned professionals.

Martin Haberman (2003), a distinguished professor at the University of Wisconsin in Milwaukee, authored a very lengthy article on urban education titled "Who Benefits from Failing Urban School Districts?" In the article, he weighed in on how the tenure of school superintendents is impacted by board actions. In it, he stated that the real reason superintendents resign or get fired is "because they have not helped the particular faction of the school board or central office staff in power at the time to gain greater resources and/or authority within the dysfunctional bureaucracy" (pp. 4). This is a profound statement that ought to give pause to everyone in the realm of district governance.

It is important to note that even though the image of the superintendent that has been painted above is of a weak administrator who is at the mercy of the board, Greene (1992) did note in his original piece, and again in his written review of the dissertation, that "the influence of board style is circumscribed by the influence of the superintendent. They are the recognized technical experts with substantial financial and staff resources, and they often control the flow of information to the board. Consequently, the board is often in a weak position to challenge the superintendent. Put another way, the board can have influence, but at the margins" (p. 221).

It should be noted that this counterbalancing of internal power was also broached in the preceding section in which the power, foresight, and vision of certain superintendents were touted because of their extraordinary achievements in their respective districts; these achievements occurred in spite of board style. Therefore, this contrasted image of a strong superintendent is relevant in this study and merits further and careful attention.

Hidden agendas: Subordination of educational goals and objectives

There are other recorded examples of boards that have various agendas aimed at serving only their personal, political, and constituent interests. Bryant and Grady (1990), for instance, noted that, "in one case, a board member allegedly sought to ruin the reputation of an unpopular elementary school teacher by bringing evidence to board meetings about the teacher. Former school teachers who were fired from their jobs and other employees serving on the board constituted another group. Their fixed purpose usually was to get rid of the superintendent who had done the firing" (p. 21). It seems reasonable, therefore, to suggest that each of these actions was motivated by personal agendas rather than by a desire to further the cause of teaching and learning. These styles of operation are liable to have some impact on the dynamics of district governance.

Along the same lines of board members with personal agendas, Rada (1988) and Stone (1988, p. 13) advanced a "candidate's calculus theory" and a "theory of policy politics," respectively. The two theories suggest that people are motivated to run for public office because of a reasoned calculation of the benefits they will derive from it—namely, prestige, power, income, and perks. If this perspective is true, then it would be reasonable to expect or suggest that those personal and intrinsic motivations may, in turn, affect the way board members deal with the school administration. They may, for instance, insist on certain policy perspectives, not for their educational value but for the resultant personal benefits: prestige, power, income, and perks.

To better underscore the differential impact of the two kinds of boards, a comparative summary table showing behavioral propensities and actual behaviors of school board members is provided. The information has been culled from the various policy-making models reviewed above and has been presented in table format below to draw a sharper comparative distinction between the actions of the two kinds of boards. In reviewing the table, the reader is urged to ask: How might a board or board members who act this way affect district governance or district performance? The table consists of two columns: the column on the left contains the views and behaviors of professional boards; the column on the right contains the views and behaviors of political boards. Each information bullet is listed under the name of the model's proponent.

Table 1

Ikejiaku's compilation of depictions and theories of school board policy-making styles from a review of the education literature

Right Way	Wrong Way
Greene, 1992	
Professional	**Political**
Views educational policy-making "as primarily a technical, expertise-based process" and relies heavily on the recommendations of the superintendent	Views role as representative of community interest; bargains with the superintendent
	Asserts authority and assumes responsibility for agenda setting
Blanchard, 1975	
Unipolar	**Bipolar**
Has less conflict and little or no identifiable blocs	Experiences substantial conflict and forms identifiable blocs or cliques
More unanimous voting behavior	Engages in more nonunanimous voting behavior along ideological lines
Lutz and Gresson, 1980	
Elite	**Arena**
Views role as guardian or trustees of the educational system	Views role as representative of segments/factions of the public
Thinks of itself as a "ruling oligarchy" that is removed from, and is aloof to, the general public	Views itself as representing a strong community life
Governs only in special areas of district governance	Governs more broadly
Thinks of itself as the guardian of the public	Nonunanimous voting behavior
Has positive, trusting, and harmonious relationship with the superintendent	Is often at loggerheads with the superintendent
Engenders or experiences few conflict situations in the running of the district	Encounters more conflict situations than the average board
	Puts pressure on the superintendent; turnover caused by arbitrary salary reduction

Table 1 (Continued)

Ikejiaku's compilation of depictions and theories of school board policy-making styles from a review of the education literature

Right Way	Wrong Way
Tallerico, 1989	
Passive-Acquiescent	**Restive-Vigilant**
Relies totally on the superintendent and trusts his or her judgment and advice	Relies less on the superintendent and more on its constituency
Does not get involved in the school system's activities	Oversees the school system with vigor
Reads and processes information from the administrative staff	Eager to question superintendent's information/advice and is ready to apply a brake to administrative activities
Katz, 1993	
Corporate	**Familial**
Has rational, predictable, and data based decision making processes	Has more personalized and affective decision making processes
Thrives on carefully developed informational reports	Is strongly influenced by personal communication and recent feedback
Has sophisticated understanding of policy and its execution, and communicates through the chain of command	Is less predictable, and less reliant on data
Prefers goal-setting, long-range planning and management by objectives as a basis for operations	Thrives on informal and oral communication, one-to-one and as a group, (he or she is suspicious of published reports with tables and appendices)
Is committed to "standards" or "excellence" rather than loyalty to a community	Not a "reading" board, but a "talking and listening" board
Values expert opinion and outside consultation	Has a flexible and situational approach to policy and its execution

Table 1 (Continued)

Ikejiaku's compilation of depictions and theories of school board policy-making styles from a review of the education literature

Right Way	Wrong Way
Katz, 1993 (Continued)	
Corporate	**Familial**
Evokes the image of a corporate board meeting in its data drenched boardroom, providing policy and oversight for a large and diverse company	Places a value on oral communication that obliterates any niceties of chain-of-command
	Prefers informal, verbal approaches to planning, and prefers satisfied constituents over measured achievements
	Loyal to the community, not to abstractions of "standards" or "excellence"
	Rejects outside or expert opinion; looks inward for resources
	Evokes the image of a group of family elders meeting in a church or at the home of one of its leading members, making decisions for a loosely connected clan of cousins, children, and in-laws

CHAPTER VI

Impact of Governing Style on Student Achievement

The preceding section profiled certain school board actions that tend to impact the governance of school districts. These actions, as noted above, are invariably directed at the superintendent (i.e., district administration) who is the person charged with carrying out the policies of the board. In this section, the focus is on whether and/or how the actions of the board might ultimately impact a school district's academic performance. If, as Anderson (1992) said, there are certain board actions that cause "serious deficiencies" in a district's educational program (p. 17), then it would be worthwhile to identify such board actions and find ways of keeping them out of the educational sphere. It is important to acknowledge, again, that the impact of board style may be mitigated by a host of other outside factors (Katz, 1993; Weick, 1982), including the superintendent's adroitness in managing board relations.

The potential to weaken the academic program of the school district

In most situations that involve "meddling in district administration," the superintendent is often hindered from performing his or her job. This sometimes culminates in a direct termination or a compelled resignation of the superintendent. When this happens, an administrative void is created that can last well into the term of the succeeding superintendent. The key concern in many board meddling situations is the danger of weakening the educational program in the district (Anderson, 1992; Greene, 1990, p. 373). School districts in which school board interference is prevalent, therefore, run the risk of having a *weakened* educational program.

As to whether or how the actions of a school board might affect the district's educational program or student achievement, one needs to read the statements of Richard Mills, the former New York State commissioner of education, who wrote, "All children can learn given appropriate instructional, social, and health services. The fact that so many of our children are not learning attests to our failure to provide these necessary services." This means that a good educational policy machine is one that can create the "right environment" as well as provide all the services necessary for all children to learn. It is therefore both conceivable and arguable that some boards would succeed and others would fail at formulating (and causing to be implemented) sound educational policies that ensure learning for ALL children. It would seem that those boards that might interject self-interest, practice nepotism, or abuse their power in any way, would be more likely to fail in this regard.

The potential for unnecessary compromises in the quality of education

A study by Bryant and Grady (1990) also provides additional insight into how certain board actions might impact a school district's performance down the road. In the survey they conducted, they noted instances in which board members chose to hire a hometown favorite rather than the best candidate or "hired a principal that the superintendent did not recommend" or, in another instance, "hired the cheapest candidate" (pp. 21). Whether one is dealing with the improper hiring of teachers, principals, or other district personnel matters, the quality of the educational program in those districts is likely to be compromised in some fashion.

Other accounts of school boards getting involved in personnel matters come from Natale (1990, p. 17), who reported incidences of nepotism, patronage, and other kinds of unethical and illegal behavior by board members. Here, once again, are examples of boards abusing their power and going outside their legal role to meddle in administrative personnel matters. (Note: It should be clarified that a board's involvement in personnel is not illegal. In fact, it is the board's duty to hire the superintendent and approve his or her subsequent appointments to top district positions. A problem arises when boards become involved in the actual personnel selection/screening process, which is the superintendent's purview.) The ultimate impact of these kinds of involvement in district personnel may manifest themselves at the district performance level. And, if this happens, student performance is likely to suffer in the hands of unqualified teachers and administrators who were hired unethically or illegally due to board influences.

Whether it is the patronage mill that was mentioned in California, the hiring of friends and family of board members in New York, or the instances of nepotism and patronage in Kentucky, district personnel administration, which ties directly to instructional programs, is bound to suffer. If incompetent people are hired, the work either does not get done, or it is done in such a shoddy manner that it harms the educational program.

The potential to create a void in the educational leadership of the district

School board styles or actions that impact superintendent tenure also deserve careful consideration, especially because there is evidence of a connection between superintendent tenure and district performance (IEL, 1986). The role of the superintendent is very vital to the smooth operation of the school district. This means that any threat to, infringement upon, or interference with this role can be potentially disastrous for a school district. Furthermore, if the interference results in a superintendent turnover (i.e., disruption in district governance), then the consequences are likely to be far more severe.

The IEL (1986) characterized the negative impact of superintendent turnover on district governance as follows: "Long periods of time without a chief executive can create problems which lie in wait for a new superintendent" because such a void lures or tempts board members into wanting to run things themselves. The IEL further notes that without a superintendent, all too often "central staff are without direction or possibly have too many directions." In other words, with a *revolving-door* superintendency, the district's goals, objectives, and priorities do not get a chance to be fully formed, tested, or implemented by a consistent leader. Instead, transient leaders, who are often at the beginning of their learning curve, tend to muddle their way through, making potentially harmful mistakes along the way. This can cause the district to flounder and lose focus of its mission, goals, and management objectives.

<u>CHAPTER VII</u>

Analysis and Discussion of the Study: Relevance to Educational Practice

This chapter provides me with the opportunity to reflect on the outcomes of this study and to put them into the proper context relative to educational practice.

Discussion

As noted in the theoretical framework discussed in Chapter IV above, this study was inspired by Greene's (1992) work on school boards in which he determined that political boards were more likely than professional boards to get involved in administrative matters, particularly in the area of personnel management. My own research essentially picked up from where Greene left off to examine whether the actions of school boards at the governance level set off a chain of events or reactions that might ultimately affect the educational performance in the district.

Given the totality of the observations made in the study, the outcome was characterized as having yielded a mixed, albeit interesting, set of results relative to style classification and student performance. For instance, there was a preponderance of professional boards in the statewide, suburban, and rural samples, but not in the urban sample. Also, the professional style registered some achievement gains in the statewide, urban, and rural samples, but not in the suburban category.

The outcome in the statewide sample was substantially consistent with the general viewpoints developed in the literature review, given that it yielded a preponderance of professional boards having higher academic performance indicators. If this statewide sample had been the only unit of analysis in the study, then the question of whether board style affects educational outcomes would have been largely answered. But by analyzing the data in smaller units (i.e., by district type), the unique characteristics of each district level surfaced, revealing a mix of outcomes that would have been masked by lumping them together.

The professional-political style splits

Based on what the literature says about the divergent beliefs and behaviors of the two groups of school boards, the outcomes noted in the statewide sample above would mean that 63% (i.e. professional) of the boards "view educational policy-making as primarily a technical, expertise-based process and therefore rely heavily on the recommendations of the superintendent, whereas 37% (i.e. political) of them view the process as one in which the board represents community interests and bargains with the superintendent" (Greene, 1992, p. 223; see also Lutz & Gresson, 1980; Tucker & Zeigler, 1980).

It is worth noting that the 63% to 37% style split that was found in the statewide sample of this study resembles Greene's (1992) 61% to 39% split in his study of New Jersey school boards. This type of consistency in outcomes may be a function of the proximity of the two states to each other and may be suggestive of common regional approaches and views about education. It would therefore be interesting to see what the replication of the same style classification would reveal in other states or regions across the country.

One thing that would have been deduced from the style splits in this study is whether or not there has been a shift toward increasing "politicization" of education, as previous research suggests. But, because this would be the first such study conducted in New York State, it essentially establishes the benchmark for the style split—not only for the statewide sample but also for the various district categories.

The impact of style on educational performance outcomes

The pattern of outcomes in the statewide, urban, and rural samples were enough to raise certain curiosities that there might be some interaction between policy-making style and educational performance that is probably not being fully captured by the style classification method. But, as plausible as this proposition may sound, there is the recognition that other extraneous factors may also be affecting the outcomes in some fashion.

For instance, the design of the instrument survey (i.e., the absence of a scaling index for "typicality" or "*atypicality*" of a district on a given policy-making style) is such that it may never yield too many statistically significant differences between the two styles. This is because every district in the sample pool, regardless of how typical they are of the policy-making styles, was included in the sample pool. This means that the performance indicators for the districts, including those that are middle-of-the-roaders, are all part of the mix, and they will tend to water down the strength of any potential differences between the styles. The challenge, therefore, lies in finding other grouping or classification mechanisms that would better isolate school districts according to how well they typify and/or exemplify each style.

An effort to test only the exemplars was made later in the study with interesting results. School districts that gave all "professional" answers and those that gave all "political" answers in response to the survey were culled from the pool and tested separately to see if being at the extremes of the two styles made any difference with respect to district performance. As shown in Table 2, the results favored the professional style as follows: the number of items with statistically significant differences increased by 5 additional items in the statewide sample; it doubled in the urban sample by an additional 10 indicators and decreased in the rural sample by 4 items. There was still no change in the suburban category.

Table 2

A comparison of the number of statistically significant items between the "conventional" and "exemplar" style classification methods

District Type	*N*=25 Conventional	*N*=36 Exemplar	Difference
Statewide	8	13	+5
Urban	10	20	+10
Suburban	0	0	0
Rural	7	3	-4

Note: All the statistically significant differences occurred in the professional sample.

Here, once again, the interpretation of the results should be conducted with caution for the reasons discussed above (i.e., the potential presence of other mitigating factors). One interesting pattern, however, is that the differences appear to increase or decrease based on the representativeness of the survey pool and study pool of the various samples. The urban sample, of course, had the highest of both measures and registered the greatest shift. The rural category followed but went in the opposite direction. As suggested above, this area warrants further examination.

The fact that the statistically significant differences in performance occurred almost exclusively in the Regents component merits some discussion. This could be attributable, in part, to the fact that the Regents testing component is the official statewide test that calls for a much higher standard than the local tests and examinations. (Note: the "advanced placement" course system is a lot more challenging and tougher than the Regents test, but it is not part of NYSED's report card system.) It would appear that the Regents component is essentially, to borrow from a popular cliché, "what separates the men from the boys." Consequently, the differences in performance in this area, especially those that are statistically significant, are deemed to be meaningful and potentially suggestive of a differential impact of style on student achievement.

The comparison of the two styles with New York State data set was equally an important aspect of this analysis, especially because it is used by experts and nonexperts alike in assessing school districts. As noted above, the idea was to see if there are differences between the two groups (professional and political) along each of the academic achievement indicators and then compare the results with New York State averages. If style were truly critical in affecting student performance, then the performance outcome of the groups should differ in terms of how they compare with the state's aggregate, with the high-performance group coming in above the state's average and the low-performing districts placing below it. The data above showed that more of the professional indicators tended to be above the state's average, and the political indicators tended to fall below in the urban and rural samples, but not in the suburban sample.

The suburban exceptions in this study are worth noting. Here, the political districts tended to slightly outperform the professional districts in a number of areas. In the observation made by Greene (2000), the reason for this type of outcome may have to do with the community pressure on suburban board members to provide quality education, irrespective of group or personal style. In any further investigation of this pattern of outcome, however, the research design ought to take into account the unique characteristics of the suburban category (size, dominant policy-making style, board and superintendent tenure, income, gender, etc.) to see if they would offer any worthwhile insights or clues on the unique outcomes in this category.

The suburban district phenomenon

As noted above, the outcome in the suburban sample was the same as in the statewide and rural samples with respect to style splits, but it was inconsistent with the rest of the samples relative to the district performance. Also, in areas where small differences were found (i.e., differences that were not statistically significant), it was the political group that performed better than the professional group.

A number of factors might have led to this unique outcome. Among them is the fact that both the percentage of the suburban population surveyed (22.5%) and the percentage of the districts that actually responded (14.0%) were both low compared to the other sample categories; however, it is not clear in which direction this might have swung the outcome. It should be noted that this does not constitute a methodological flaw in the study, but rather, it is a built-in weakness in the field of inferential statistics.

Greene (2000) weighed in on the suburban outcome during his review of the dissertation manuscript and suggested that the reason why there is little influence of board style on performance in the suburbs, particularly wealthier ones, is that the pressure on the suburban school district to provide a quality education is quite enormous, and most board members will reflect this community view. Hence, even though there may be different board styles, there may be little disagreement among board members over the direction of the district.

There are a few other possible explanations—not answers—for the suburban phenomenon, including the possibility that board style does not really have any impact on performance, and the possibility that any such impact may be mitigated by other factors. Once again, these are only speculations that call for validation in future research.

Implications of the study

The results of this study might have some implications in terms of the views, beliefs, and behaviors of school boards as well as on the context in which they occur. Specifically, they could imply the following:

> First, that there are more professional boards in the statewide, suburban, and rural categories than in the urban category. These are boards that, according to information in the literature that was reviewed, see educational policy making as one that is "primarily a technical, expertise-based process" that relies heavily on the recommendations of the superintendent; meddles very little in district administration, and potentially helps to engender higher student achievement in the district.
>
> Second, the language of the education laws in many states (including New York State, where the study was conducted), is very vague and may be partly responsible for the confusion on board-superintendent roles. The vagueness often leads to both honest and politically motivated encroachments on each other's turf (the board's and the superintendent's). The various school district reform efforts being undertaken by some municipal governments underscore the vagueness of the state education laws.

> Third, from a reform perspective, knowing that a certain aspect of a district's educational performance might be based on its policy-making style is good news because it means that through training and board development, a failing district would have a chance of being turned around. This avenue of hope would not exist if performance is linked exclusively to such situational or environmental factors as socioeconomic status.

Put another way, if district performance is associated with the style of the board, then there is hope that minds and behaviors of school boards can be changed through training and board development programs. Given the outcome of this study, it would mean that the urban and rural samples would be trained and/or redirected more toward the professional policy-making style, while the suburban group would either be left alone or encouraged to adopt the political style.

CHAPTER VIII

Recommendations

As indicated above, it is important to characterize this study and the new ground it covered on student achievement as exploratory but highly instructive. It would, therefore, benefit from further research into its major concepts and methodology. However, based on the outcomes and the lessons learned from the study, a few recommendations have been put forward for a wider audience of readers and stakeholders. The original set of recommendations from the study has also been included here for reference purposes as chapter XVI.

Recommendations for stakeholders

1. Engage all stakeholders, including state departments of education, to devise and standardize certain governing style indicators for school districts. This would help in the monitoring and redirecting of the policy-making styles of school boards. This recommendation essentially recognizes the fact that the control of school districts is the ultimate responsibility of the state government, even though it is structurally delegated to local communities. If it turns out that a board's policy-making style impacts its educational performance in some fashion, it would behoove the stakeholders to become major players in changing people's mindset and redirecting school boards toward adopting a style, or mix of styles, that works.

2. Call upon state departments of education to review their education laws for vagueness, especially because a lack of clarity is often blamed for the confusion on board-superintendent roles. A clearly defined set of roles and expectations for school boards and superintendents would help to reduce conflict and turf wars between the two key players.

3. Require training for all new and sitting members of the school board to help them understand the role of the board. Thankfully, this is now happening in many states across the country and would hopefully become a national expectation or even a requirement across the country.

Suggestions for further study

For anyone looking to replicate, improve upon, or simply use this study as part of a conceptual framework, a few suggestions are in order. Specifically, the prospective researcher should consider the following:

1. Modify Greene's (1992) classification system slightly so that it can produce groupings of school districts not only by the two policy-making styles but also by how well each district typifies a given policy-making style. This is what I have called the "exemplar system," by which a district is rated on a scale of 1 to 2 for each style on how well it typifies that particular style. This would yield such groupings as "professional 1 or 2" and "political 1 or 2," depending on how well those districts typify the policy-making style, with "1" being the best fit and "2" being a loose fit. As noted above, the attempt was made in this study to

compare the performance of an "all-professional" pool with that of an "all-political" pool, which yielded some interesting outcomes.

2. Doing a mix of quantitative and qualitative analysis with respect to classifying boards by their policy-making style. This would undoubtedly take a longer time to conduct and would cost more money, but it would yield additional useful information. Such an expanded study could entail doing surveys, interviews, and field observations as well as traveling and the use of certain monitoring equipment. The major benefit to this comprehensive approach would be to guard against the potential for board presidents to under—or overreport certain situations in the district, either purposely or due to a lack of knowledge.

3. If resources allow, it may behoove the next researcher also to investigate the superintendent's role in the governance dynamics. Recall that Katz (1993) theorized that district dynamics is a function of the right "match-up" between the board and the superintendent. The challenge here lies in operationalizing and quantifying the style of the superintendent so that it can be measured either qualitatively or quantitatively. This set of information and those that would be obtained from the school board would then be manipulated to measure their impact.

4. It might also be worthwhile to conduct this study in all 50 states, either through sampling or by a study of the entire school board population. This would yield conclusions that are potentially generalizable to the nation as a whole. Furthermore, and as indicated above, it will show the various splits in terms of professional and political styles and, by so doing, reveal the

various subject areas, as well as parts of the country, that may require special attention.

5. It would be worthwhile to pay more attention to the suburban districts because of their unique performance outcomes in the study. This should include an initial examination of the unique characteristics of the suburban category (size, dominant policy-making style, board and superintendent tenure, income, gender, etc.) to better pin down the specific variable, or group of variables, that underlies their higher performance over the rest of the districts' categories as well as the apparent absence of the impact of style on educational outcomes.

6. Recognizing the potential for distortion in the district assessment methodology, it might be worthwhile to conduct the academic performance analysis by separating out the three Regents criteria for an in-depth review. If this isolation approach changes the outcome of any such study substantially, then it would confirm the suspicion that the current system is flawed.

7. Even though the potential role of SES in the study was deemed to be minimal, it would still be worthwhile to continue to investigate the degree to which it is associated with student performance. Specifically, it might be worthwhile to perform a regression analysis on SES, board style, and performance indicators to see if they are (and if so, how they might be) related.

8. In addition to examining the impact of SES, future research might also benefit from a look at a measure of community/parent education level as an independent variable.

This may be a better measure of community support/interest in education than SES. Admittedly, this type of analysis may be difficult because the information may not be broken down by school district.

9. One final suggestion: If the data on per-pupil expenditures are available, it might be worthwhile to study the possible correlation or association of board style to expenditures. It is likely that professional boards may spend more because they may want to support quality education, and political boards may spend less because of taxpayer and parental pressures.

CHAPTER IX

Implications for Board Orientation, Training, and Professional Development

Serving on school boards is a noble and commendable civic act. Those who are currently serving or are aspiring to serve should be commended for wanting to get involved because it is hard work, and is getting harder and harder with each passing day. Boards have very little ability to control many of the challenges and dilemmas they encounter on a daily basis (shrinking financial resources, stiff global competition on academic achievement, growing social and economic pressures on families and students, etc.). However, they can do a few things differently to ensure the smooth running of their districts, including *"learning to govern"* the right way.

In order to learn to govern the right way, it behooves school boards and/or individual board members across the country to (a) become more knowledgeable about their role in district governance, (b) become knowledgeable about the history and role of school boards, (c) learn about the various policy-making styles that school boards adopt, and (d) become aware of how those governing styles impact district administration and, ultimately, student achievement.

It should be noted that a number of states, (Texas, New York, Illinois, and many others), are now requiring training and ongoing professional development for board members through a number of legislative mandates in education reform. This new emphasis across the country on the need for preservice board training is, in essence, a tacit acknowledgment that *knowing how to govern a school district* is very important! By logical extension, this means that the governing style of school boards can be a factor in the way school districts are governed and that it can ultimately impact student achievement.

Learning objectives and training modules

Based on the points made above, a meaningful set of ***learning objectives*** for board orientation, training, and development ought to encompass the following:

MODULE A
The origins, history, and role of school boards
(Chapters I and II)

- Learn about the origins and history of the school board form of district governance

- Learn about the qualifications for being a board member

- Learn about the proper ***motivations*** and ***roles*** of school boards within the district governance context

MODULE B

A review of the various policy-making or governing styles (Chapter III)

- Understand that school boards have unique governing styles that could either hurt or help their district

- Reflect on personal beliefs and "governing style" to determine if the board or a board member operates in a ***professional*** or ***political*** manner

MODULE C

How the policy-making styles impact district administration (Chapters IV and V)

- Learn about how those unique styles can affect the administration of the district (board-superintendent relations). This includes learning about the deleterious effects of not "staying in one's lane" with regard to district administration

MODULE D

The impact of board policy-making style on student achievement (Chapters IV and VI)

- Learn about how ***student achievement*** can be impacted as a result of what happens with the governing style of school boards

MODULE E

Personal and professional reflections (Chapters VII and VIII)

- Reflect on personal experiences and observations as a prospective, current, or former board member

CHAPTER X

Noteworthy Information from the Study—Extra, Extra!

Part of the information obtained through the study, such as superintendent tenure, types of district conflicts, board member tenure, and president's tenure as well as gender, education, and family income of the board members, are compiled and summarized here for the reader as follows:

A. Introduction

B. Respondent characteristics
   1. Analysis by policy-making style
   2. Analysis by district type
   3. Board member tenure
   4. Board president's tenure
   5. Gender
   6. Education
   7. Annual family income

C. Superintendent tenure
   1. Analysis by policy-making style
   2. Analysis by district type

D. District conflicts/controversies
   1. Analysis by policy-making style
   2. Analysis by district type

E. Summary

A INTRODUCTION

The data source for this analysis was the 67, or 42.1%, of the 159 responses obtained from the longer version of the survey. Many of the respondents did not volunteer information on all the personal information items, especially on educational attainment and family income. In one case, a respondent wrote: "Sorry, question not appropriate" in response to the family income question. But the few who chose to respond provided enough information to be used to conduct the analysis. It should be noted that this information ties in—and is consistent—with the discussion on board characteristics and superintendent tenure in the literature review section of the actual study.

The analysis included the following: (1) information on how long respondents have been serving as board members, (2) how long they have been serving as board president, (3) their gender, (4) their level of educational attainment, (5) their family income, (6) information on how long the current superintendent has been in office, and (7) the existence and nature of district conflicts/controversies.

B. RESPONDENT CHARACTERISTICS

1. Analysis by policy-making style

As the data in Table AA-1 show, respondents from professional districts reported slightly longer board tenure than those from political districts. But because there are too many potential unknowns in the responses, no substantive conclusions were drawn from the outcomes. It should be noted, however, that this outcome is consistent with the body of knowledge in the school board literature. The references to the body of literature on this topic overwhelmingly ascribe low conflict, low controversies, and low turnover to professional boards. On the other hand, political boards, which are often burdened by board-superintendent conflicts, political activism, and the like, tend to be more prone to higher turnover.

Table AA-1

Characteristics of the respondents: average tenure, gender, educational attainment, and family income.

#	Indicators	Prof.	Pol.
1	Average tenure of respondents as board members (in years)	[9.4]	7.0
2	Average tenure of respondents as board presidents (in years)	3.5	3.5
3	Gender of respondents		
	a. Number of male respondents	[30]	16
	b. Number of female respondents	[15]	6
4	Average educational attainment of respondents	College degree	College degree
5	Average family income of respondents	$50-$75k	$50-$75k

[ ] Indicates a higher numerical value

The table above shows that there are more males (46, or 68.7%) in board service than females (21, or 31.3%). The table also shows that 45, or 67.2%, of all the respondents were from professional districts, while the remaining 22, or 32.8%, belonged to political districts. Of the 45 respondents from professional districts, 30, or 66.7%, were male and 15, or 33.3%, were female. Finally, of the 22 respondents from political districts, 16, or 72.7%, were male, while 6, or 27.3%, were female.

2. Analysis by district type

In addition to the macro-summary presented above, there is also a micro-summary of the respondent characteristics presented in Table AA-2 below. It should be noted that the analysis here did not include the responses from the Big 4 urban districts (Buffalo, Rochester, Syracuse, and Yonkers) because of the potential for skewing the results.

Table AA-2

Characteristics of respondents: tenure, gender, educational attainment, and family income, presented by district type.

#	District Type	Average tenure as board members (in years)	Average tenure as board president (in years)	Gender		Educational attainment	Average family income ($000s)
1	Urban (N=16)	7.1	2.5	Male =9	Female=7	Graduate work	$75k+
2	Suburban (N=27)	9.0	3.6	Male =21	Female=6	College degree	$50-$75k
3	Rural (N=23)	9.2	4.1	Male =15	Female=8	College degree	$50-$75k

a. Tenure as a board member—Respondents from suburban and rural districts reported serving longer terms as "board members" than those from urban districts.

b. Tenure as a board president—Respondents from rural and suburban districts also reported serving slightly longer terms as "board president" than those from urban districts. This means that the rural and suburban respondents serve about three 2-year terms, while those from urban districts serve less than that.

c. Gender—In terms of proportional representation in each district category, the urban district category appears to have the highest percentage of female board members and board presidents (43.8%), compared to the rural (34.8%) and suburban (22.2%) districts.

d. Education—Respondents from urban districts reported a slightly higher level of educational attainment (i.e., graduate work), while those from suburban and rural districts reported holding mostly baccalaureates.

e. Annual family income—Respondents from urban districts reported earning substantially higher family incomes than their counterparts in the suburban and rural districts. (Note: the income source is not exclusive to the respondents' jobs as board members and/or board presidents.)

C. SUPERINTENDENT TENURE

1. Analysis by policy-making style

As the data in Table AA-3 show, respondents from professional districts reported slightly longer superintendent tenure than their counterparts from political districts. But, as was noted above, no conclusions were drawn from this outcome because of too many unknowns in the data returns. For example, while some superintendents may leave their district because they feel burdened and beleaguered by their school board, others leave in pursuit of "greener pastures" elsewhere or simply retire after serving out their term in office. Therefore, unless the split on "voluntary" and "involuntary" superintendent departures can be determined, no meaningful conclusions can be drawn from the outcome. And even so, reports of voluntary superintendent separation need to be thoroughly verified to make sure a forcible removal is not masked by a mutual separation agreement that holds both parties harmless in times of contract liability.

Table AA-3

Summary of respondent and other district characteristics on tenure, gender, educational attainment, and family income

Indicator	Professional	Political
Average superintendent tenure reported by respondents (in years)	[5.6]	4.6

[ ] Indicates a higher numerical value

It is worth noting here as well that the longer superintendent tenure reported by respondents in the professional districts is also consistent with the body of knowledge in the school board literature, especially with regard to how a superintendent's tenure can be closely tied to the kind of relationship he or she has with the board.

2. Analysis by district type

A review of the information by district type shows that superintendents appear to stay about five years, regardless of the type of district, although those in rural districts seem to stay a little longer. The reported average length of service for superintendents in the various districts is as follows: 5.0 years for the urban districts, 5.1 years for the suburban districts, and 5.6 years for the rural districts. It should be noted that there were wide variations in the raw data on superintendent tenure, ranging from as little as 6 months up to 19 years.

D. DISTRICT CONFLICTS/CONTROVERSIES

1. Analysis by policy-making style

Of the 67 board presidents who completed the long survey, 40 (or 59.7%), reported various types of recent controversies in their districts. The bulk of the controversies were reported by respondents from professional districts. Specifically, of the 40 respondents, 25 (or 62.5%), were from professional districts, while 15 (or 37.5%), were from political districts. Whether this difference is real or simply reflects a difference in the propensity to report controversies could not be determined from the available data.

Table AA-4 contains a listing of 59 different types of controversies arranged by district category. The types of issues run the gamut, but a few of them popped up more often than others: transportation topped the list with six mentions, sports programs were mentioned five times, and grade reconfiguration was mentioned four times. Six other items were mentioned at least twice: coaching matters, district mergers, drugs and alcohol policies, health/safety issues (bomb and gun threats), student discipline, and use of school facilities.

All three district types reported about the same number of controversies. For instance, of the 59 controversies reported, 20, or 33.9%, were from respondents in the urban districts; 21, or 35.6%, were from suburban districts; and 18, or 30.5%, were from the rural districts. Within each district category, however, there were some wild splits in the number of items reported by each policy-making style. In the urban category, the political group reported 17, or 35.0%, of the 20 items, whereas in the suburban and rural categories, the professional group reported 16, or 76.2%, of the 21 items and 13, or 72.2%, of the 18 items, respectively.

2. Analysis by district type

A review of the district conflicts/controversies by district type is presented below:

#	**Type of controversy**

Urban districts

1. Academic disability standards for extracurricular activities
2. Academic standards
3. Class size
4. Coaching
5. Continuation of some honors programs in the district
6. Drug abatement
7. Elimination of in-house ROTC program
8. Financial issues—budget and contract negotiations
9. Grade reconfiguration
10. Hiring superintendent
11. Public safety—drug searches with police dogs
12. Redistricting of elementary schools
13. Special education
14. Student graduation requirements
15. Superintendent independent authority to hire senior aides
16. Transportation
17. Violence reduction

Suburban districts

1. Capital projects
2. Coaching—hiring policy
3. Curriculum
4. District hiring policy
5. District merger
6. Environmental cleanup
7. Facility maintenance/upgrade
8. Gifted children's program

9. Grade reconfiguration
10. Personnel—bus driver and student conduct
11. Personnel—no confidence vote on a secondary principal
12. Sports
13. Student discipline
14. Student reassignment to another class
15. Student's right to curriculum choice
16. Transportation
17. Weather-related school closing

Rural districts

1. Book selection/access
2. District merger
3. Drug and alcohol policies
4. Grading
5. Guidelines on executive session matters
6. Health/safety—bomb and gun threats
7. Health/safety—emergency response
8. Homeschooler participation in regular school programs
9. Lunch room policy
10. New construction
11. Sports
12. Student privileges
13. Student trespassers
14. Transportation
15. Use of facilities

E. SUMMARY

Respondents from professional districts reported having served longer terms as board members over their counterparts from political districts. No difference was found between the two styles on the respondents' length of service as board president. Respondents from rural and suburban districts reported slightly longer terms as "board members" than those from the urban districts. But respondents from urban districts, on the other hand, reported higher levels of educational attainment and family income as well as a higher percentage of female members/presidents over the suburban and rural districts.

With regard to superintendent tenure, respondents from professional districts reported a slightly longer tenure for their superintendents than those from political districts. As was the case above, there was little or no difference in the length of superintendent tenure between the three district types. However, the rural districts reported a slightly higher average than the others.

Finally, the bulk of the district conflicts/controversies occurred mostly in professional districts. Transportation, sports, and grade reconfiguration came up as the most often cited causes of district conflict.

CHAPTER XI

Important *Takeaways*

I want to begin this chapter by thanking the reader for finding this book important or interesting enough to read it. I want to leave you with a few *takeaways* that I believe are critical in this discussion.

First, the doctoral dissertation that gave rise to this book is part of a recent wave of research efforts linking *governing style to student achievement*. This research effort shows that the list of what ails public education is usually long, but seldom includes the governing style of school boards—a critical omission in the education literature!

Second, and per the doctoral research I conducted, majority of the boards in the statewide study sample, as well as those in the suburban and rural samples tend to govern in a "professional" manner, while those in urban districts govern in a "political" manner. Also, student achievement outcomes in districts with professional boards were generally higher than the performance outcomes of districts with political boards, except in the suburban category where the result was mixed. The greatest effect was observed in the urban district category which has a preponderance of the political style and lower achievement outcomes.

Third, the role of school boards is policy-making and any other statutorily outlined duties, while district administration is the sole province of the superintendent. School boards are supposed to (1) function as trustees of education with no allegiance whatsoever to those who appoint or elect them; (2) ensure that the educational environment in their districts adequately "serves the needs of the learners;" (3) given their lay backgrounds, they are supposed to defer to the expertise of the superintendent on administrative and educational matters; (4) avoid partisan politics and not become involved in the day-to-day administration of school districts; and (5) set educational policy and ensure that the schools are well-run by the superintendent.

Fourth, every school board adopts a certain *governing style* once it is constituted, and the adopted governing style invariably impacts the internal dynamics of district administration. This means that whichever governing style a board adopts is likely to impact district administration and ultimately have a domino effect on student achievement.

Fifth, as the saying goes, "behavior has consequences!" How a school board governs a school district is bound to impact how things turn out. If a board governs well, the district will experience positive results; if it governs badly, the negative effects will be felt.

Sixth, technically, the board really only hires the superintendent, who in turn is responsible for hiring and recommending the balance of the district staff to the board for approval. This means that if there are problems or disagreements between the board and the superintendent regarding personnel administration, it is time for introspection.

Seventh, superintendents should be held accountable for *clearly defined* performance objectives and outcomes. After all they are hired because they are the educational experts. In fact, the expense and rigorous process for hiring superintendents are clues that they are important to the operation of the district. In fact, the phrase "Chief Executive Officer" is at times used interchangeably for superintendents, and appropriately so. If a superintendent is prevented from performing according to what he or she knows, then the purpose for hiring him/her has been defeated.

Eighth, if a board finds that it is often at odds with its superintendent, it is time to engage in soul searching and introspection about how it is going about its governance role. More importantly, it should seek out an opportunity to discuss the issues among its members or better yet, call for a professional development session.

Ninth, if a board realizes that it is making decisions (voting behavior) along any ideologies or political lines, it ought to be cause for concern. This is because a good idea is a good idea regardless of who it comes from. And so, if these types of divisions emerge on the board, it is time for introspection or professional development.

Tenth and finally, each of the good board governance behaviors that is described in this book ought to be copied by ALL categories of school districts. But more importantly, the fact that the *political* governing style is more prevalent in urban districts, and correlates with low student achievement, ought to be cause for concern in urban districts.

Note to the reader!

Congratulations on finishing Part One. Parts two and three contain additional technical information and details of the study that were excerpted from the dissertation. Please *read on!*

PART TWO

CHAPTER XII

Study Methodology

This study was conducted in two distinct phases. Phase I involved the surveying of school board presidents to gather information on the views and actions of their boards, which, in turn, formed the basis for classifying the boards according to their policy-making styles. The selection of school districts was made in a stratified, random fashion so as to give all districts and district types (i.e., urban, suburban, and rural) equal chance of being selected. Depending on the board president's responses to three key questions on the survey, the districts were classified as either "professional" or "political" in accordance with Greene's (1992) classification model.

Phase II of the study involved the compilation and manipulation of student achievement data on all the districts in the sample pool using the 1998 edition of the New York State School District Report Card; this information is published annually by the New York State Education Department (NYSED). Descriptive and aggregate statistical data for each group of school districts were manipulated and compared. The ultimate goal was to determine whether there are differences in the student achievement indicators of the professional and political districts, and if so, whether the differences are statistically significant at the .05 alpha level. There was also an effort in this phase to examine the potential connection between SES and board style, which would, in turn, imply an indirect role for poverty in educational outcomes via board orientation.

A. Description of the Respondents

The respondents were 258 school board presidents from a total of 51 counties in New York State's public school districts. The choice of board presidents as the source of this information was based on the fact that "they are elected by their colleagues and thus tend to be representative of members' orientations and behaviors. [And] they are also likely to have more information and insight into board activities" (Greene, 1992, p. 222). They are, therefore, the most reliable and credible source of information on how their boards operate.

B. Study Variables

The variables in this study are defined and operationalized below.

1. Independent Variables (Defined and Operationalized)

The independent variables were operationalized by the two policy-making styles: "professional" and "political." These two labels represent the distinguishing characteristics of the two populations that are under study. As indicated above, the policy-making styles were determined using Greene's (1992) survey classification method described in detail in the survey instrument development section below. Also, see Greene (1992, pp. 223-225).

2. Dependent Variables (Defined and Operationalized)

The dependent variables—the characteristics that are being measured for the two samples—include four educational performance categories that contain a total of 49 student achievement indicators used by NYSED in the 1998 edition of the School District Report Card; they include: graduation/college rates

(3 items), Pupil Evaluation Program (5 items), Pupil Evaluation Tests (5 items), and Regents Examinations (12 items).

C. Survey Instrument Development

The survey instruments that were used in this study were adapted from Greene's (1992) 33-point, seven-page survey. The source survey was obtained directly from the developer, Kenneth Greene, who was contacted on August 17, 1998, to request a copy of the survey and to obtain permission to use the instrument in this study; both requests were granted. Greene was contacted again on September 4, 1998, to acknowledge receipt of the survey and to ask some follow up questions on certain details of the study that were not part of the published report. The key question was whether the source survey was piloted prior to its administration; it was piloted on 20 school district officials that included 10 board presidents and 10 superintendents.

The fact the survey was adapted from a published study that has also been in the public domain for over 8 years, lessens—but does not completely eliminate—the burden of addressing the validity and reliability issues related to this study. A critical consideration here is the threshold question of whether any differences between the source survey and the ones used in this study are likely to affect the outcome of the study. Two different types of surveys, a long and a short one, were created out of Greene's (1992) original instrument. This dual version strategy was the product of a careful consideration of the characteristics of the respondents and whether the response rate might be affected by the format of either instrument.

1. The long survey instrument

Greene's (1992) original 33-point, seven-page survey was adapted wholesale for this study and was administered to half of the sample pool, which was also stratified by district type and administered randomly within each category. For instance, within the urban district stratum, half of the districts were randomly selected (using a random number table) to complete the long version. This version contained not only the three key classification questions, but also other questions that are either tangential to the study or have an entirely different focus.

2. The short survey instrument

Upon recognizing that using all of the 33 questions from the original survey might be a bit too daunting to respondents (and, as such, could depress or inhibit response rates), a scaled-down version of the survey that has only six questions on a single page was developed and administered to the remaining half of the sample pool, also in a stratified random fashion. In the shorter version, only the relevant questions that identified the districts and their policy-making styles were included. In addition to the three demographic questions, the careful selection of the other three classification questions was guided by Greene (1992), who identified them as follows:

> The responses to three questions—how much time they spend responding to contacts, how frequently they vote unanimously, and to what extend they rely on the guidance of the superintendent—were combined to classify the boards as either professional or political.

Based on this reference, six questions were deemed relevant and were included in the short version survey (three items on district demographics and three on style classification). These items correspond to items 1, 2, 7, 14, 20, and 30 in the original survey.

This short survey, which contains 24 fewer items than the original instrument, had the added advantage of being brief and, therefore, potentially less daunting to the respondents. It also spared the respondents three potentially invasive questions that probe the respondents' gender, level of education, and family income (items 31, 32, and 33 in the source survey). It also spared respondents from answering three other potentially problematic questions on how boards relate to parents and community groups (items 8, 9, and 11); every one of the response choices to these questions can potentially be construed negatively. For example, in question number eight of the original survey, making oneself easily available or accessible to people may be construed as politicking, grandstanding, and/or upstaging the superintendent's management responsibility. On the other hand, "avoiding them" can be construed as being standoffish, aloof, arrogant, or, in an extreme sense, shirking one's board duties. Therefore, with respect to the threshold question above, one can be reasonably certain that the short survey does not differ in any substantive way, but rather, it differs only in the sheer number of survey questions. In fact, the "short and simple" appearance of this scaled-down version should be considered a far greater advantage over the 33-point version.

It should be noted that the return rates on the two versions confirmed my hunch that the long version might tend to overwhelm respondents and, by so doing, depress responses: the response rate for the shorter version was 70.8%, while the longer version was 52.3%. Extrapolated further, this means that if the long survey had been used exclusively, it would have yielded 135 responses, which is 24 less than the current rate of 159. On the other hand, if the short survey had been used exclusively, it would have yielded an additional 24 responses, increasing the number from the current rate of 159 to 183. The current split design, in essence, yielded a middle-ground return rate of 159 (or 61.6%).

Finally, given the fact that the survey instruments were derived wholly from Greene's original instrument, they benefit vicariously from the extent of its inherent validity and suffer precipitously from any demonstrable shortcomings. While no surveyor can completely overcome the hidden biases or motivations of respondents, demonstrating that such biases and motivations can be kept to a minimum is very important. The validity and reliability discussions below speak to this effort.

D. Validity

The question that is asked about the validity of any survey instrument is whether it truly assesses what it purports to measure (Fink, 1995). In the case of the source and adapted surveys, one can reasonably be assured that they meet this validity threshold, given that there is an adequate grounding of the questions in the education literature, as well as in Greene's (1992) own professional experience as a researcher and educator.

In the scaled down version of the instrument, questions one, two, and three (which correspond to 1, 2, and 30 in the source survey) are demographic pieces of information about school districts. They ask about the grade levels in each district, the student population, and whether boards are elected or appointed. As in all surveys, these demographic questions help to identify the target population and to organize and describe observations from the study.

Questions four, five, and six ask about how the board members interact with parents and community groups, how they make decisions, and how they interact with the superintendent. As Greene (1992) noted, each of these questions comes from the school board literature, which documents the existence of a variety of policy-making styles on a continuum of two extremes (Blanchard, 1975; Katz, 1993; Lutz & Gresson, 1980; Tallerico, 1989).

The questions on style classification were operationalized by Greene (1992) as follows: First, the interaction with parents and community groups, which is evidence of a board's level of responsiveness, were measured by hours of community/parental contact per week. Less than 3 hours per week would be indicative of a professional board, while 3 hours or more per week would be indicative of a political board; second, the degree of intra-board conflict was measured by percent of unanimous decisions. A percent index of 90% or more would be characteristic of a professional board while less than 90% would characterize a political board.

It should be noted that the application of inter—and intra-board conflict in measuring the style of boards is widespread among school board researchers. For instance, in two separate studies by Blanchard (1975) and Tallerico (1989), they used the presence or absence, as well as the degree of conflict, as one of the key measures in determining a board's style. Third, the question of whether the board generally believes in—and/or observes—the distinction between the policy-making role of the board and the administrative role of the superintendent. Professional boards, which tend not to seek involvement beyond their policy-making realm and rely more on the expertise of the superintendent, would agree with the proposition, while political boards, with their opposing philosophy, would tend to disagree more (Greene, 1992, p. 224).

E. Reliability

The potential for measurement error is at the heart of the reliability question (Fink, 1995). Greene (1992) made deliberate efforts to avoid measurement errors in his survey by using simple, carefully worded, complete, and conversational sentences both in the cover letter and in the survey itself. The instrument's language level is such that it significantly reduces ambiguity, and, in turn, reduces the chances of measurement error; this assumes, of course, that the hurdle of poor administration would reasonably be overcome. It should also be noted that a wide range of response choices was provided in various items in the source survey that require a judgment call from the respondent. For instance, in items 4, 6, 7, 12, and 22 in the source survey, respondents had a range of between four and five answers to choose from. This should provide ample latitude in the analysis phase in making a determination as to which half of the continuum to place a subject's answer.

F. Procedure for the Study

The study involved a number of steps and tasks that are discussed below in a sequence that helps to organize the thought process, but should not be construed as necessarily a rigid methodological sequence.

1. **Respondent Identification:** The names, addresses, and other identifying information about districts and their boards were obtained from the New York State School Boards Association (NYSSBA), a professional membership organization that maintains information about school board members in New York State. The information was verified by cross-referencing it with the directory of school districts maintained by the New York State Education Department.

   From the universe of the 706 public school districts in New York State, 258, or 36.5%, of them were randomly selected for inclusion in the study. The random selection was also stratified so as to include the three different categories or levels of school districts as follows: (1) the urban districts, which included 58 of the 61 urban districts and 4 of the Big 5 districts (Note: the Big 5 districts are Buffalo, Rochester, Syracuse, and Yonkers; New York City was excluded because of its unique configuration and an extraordinarily large student population), (2) the suburban districts from where 100 out of 444 were selected, and (3) the rural districts where 100 out of 184 were selected. The goal was to randomly select 100 samples from each category for a total of 300. But, because the urban district category has only 58 eligible districts in it, the 300 mark could not be reached; this resulted in having 258 as the final sample pool. See Table 3 below for New York State's school district demographics as well as the sample selection data for this study. It contains information on the "number" and "size" of the various district types in New York State as well as the number and percent of each district type that was surveyed.

By looking at the "% of districts surveyed" column for each district type, one can estimate the degree to which the results of the study might be generalizable to real-life situations. For instance, the outcomes should ring more true for the urban district sample that has a 95.1% representation in the survey pool than for the rural (49.8%) and the suburban (22%) samples that have less representation.

Table 3

District demographics: The number and average enrollment size of the various district types in New York State, along with information on the number and percent of each group that was surveyed

District Category	Number of Districts in New York State	Average Enrollment Size	Number of Districts Surveyed	Percent of Districts Surveyed
Urban Districts	61	4,430 *	58	95.1%
Suburban Districts	444	2,601	100	22.5%
Rural Districts	201 **	1,097	100	49.8%
Total	**706**	**N/A**	**258**	**36.5%**

Note: From 1998 School District Report Card

* Excluding the Big 5 districts (all urban but without NYC is 32,089; NYC is 1,049,873)

** Number may vary from year to year due to consolidations and/or mergers in this category.

2. **Survey Cover Letter:** The surveys were mailed to the school board presidents with individualized cover letters that identified the researcher, the research objectives, how the results would be used, and how the identity of the respondents would be protected. They also contained pledges of confidentiality in the handling of the survey responses provided.
3. **Follow-up Action:** In some instances when some board presidents did not return their survey at all or on time, reminder letters containing another copy of the survey were sent. In one or two occasions, reminder phone calls were made.

G. Data Review and Analysis

As the completed surveys were received, they were reviewed for completeness before being included in the analysis.

1. ***Study Phase I—determining a board's policy-making style***
Once a returned survey was deemed eligible for inclusion in the study pool, it was put through a screening test to determine the policy-making style of the board. Greene's (1992) "two-out-of-three" formula was used to accomplish the classification task. Districts were classified as "professional" if the board president gave at least two of the following "professional" responses: spent less than 3 hours per week responding to parents, experienced more than 90% unanimous decisions, and completely maintained the distinction between policy making and administration. Conversely, a board was classified as "political" if the president gave at least two of the following "political" responses: spent more than 3 hours

per week responding to parents, experienced less than 90% unanimous decisions, and exhibited nonrecognition of the distinction between policy making and administration (Greene, 1992, p. 224). This process yielded two different groups: "professional" and "political," which constituted the two experimental treatment conditions or independent variables.

2. *Study Phase II—comparing the groups' student achievement indicators*

Once the classification and grouping of the districts were completed, the aggregate student achievement indicators of the two groups were culled from NYSED's database and compared. The electronic version of the student achievement data was used in this study with the help of a statistical software package called Minitab, but it was augmented by Microsoft Excel spreadsheet application software. The performance of the two groups of school districts was then compared to the set of comprehensive student achievement indicators shown on Table 4 below. The table lists the four major district assessment areas and their sub-indicators.

Table 4

Summary of student achievement indicators: Core assessment areas and Regents Examinations components combined

A. Graduation Rates and Percent to College

1. Percent of Regents Diplomas for 1988/89
2. Percent of Regents Diplomas for 1996/97
3. Percent of 1995/96 to college

B. Pupil Evaluation Program (% above NYS minimum)

1. Grade 3 Reading
2. Grade 3 Math
3. Grade 5 Writing
4. Grade 6 Reading
5. Grade 6 Math

C. Program Evaluation Tests (mean scores)

1. Grade 4 Science Objective Test (Content)
2. Grade 4 Science Objective Test (Skills)
3. Grade 4 Science (Manipulative Skills)
4. Grade 6 Social Studies
5. Grade 8 Social Studies

D. Regents Examinations

1. Comprehensive English
   a. % of average grade enrollment tested
   b. % of tested passing
   c. % of average grade enrollment passing

2. Global Studies
   a. % of average grade enrollment tested
   b. % of tested passing
   c. % of average grade enrollment passing

3. U.S. History/Government
   a. % of average grade enrollment tested
   b. % of tested passing
   c. % of average grade enrollment passing

4. Comprehensive French
   a. % of average grade enrollment tested
   b. % of tested passing
   c. % of average grade enrollment passing

5. Comprehensive Spanish
   a. % of average grade enrollment tested
   b. % of tested passing
   c. % of average grade enrollment passing
6. Sequential Math 1
   a. % of average grade enrollment tested
   b. % of tested passing
   c. % of average grade enrollment passing

7. Sequential Math 2
   a. % of average grade enrollment tested
   b. % of tested passing
   c. % of average grade enrollment passing

8. Sequential Math 3
   a. % of average grade enrollment tested
   b. % of tested passing
   c. % of average grade enrollment passing

9. Earth Science-94 Ed
   a. % of average grade enrollment tested
   b. % of tested passing
   c. % of average grade enrollment passing

10. Biology
    a. % of average grade enrollment tested
    b. % of tested passing
    c. % of average grade enrollment passing

11. Chemistry
    a. % of average grade enrollment tested
    b. % of tested passing
    c. % of average grade enrollment passing

12. Physics
    a. % of average grade enrollment tested
    b. % of tested passing
    c. % of average grade enrollment passing

The **mean** and **standard deviation** of each of the 49 performance variables were computed for each of the two groups of school districts. These were, in turn, compared in various t-tests to see the following: (1) whether there are differences between the aggregate student achievement indicators of the two groups, (2) what the direction of any observed differences is, and (3) whether the differences are statistically significant. Statistical tests at the .05 alpha level were performed to determine whether differences between the two groups were significant. (Note: statistical significance, of course, means that the observed difference could not be obtained by chance in 95% of such sampling attempts.)

H. Statistical Testing and Analysis

In analyzing the data collected in this study, two different types of inferential statistical methods were used as warranted by the purpose of the study, the nature of the data collected, and the size of the samples. The statistical applications used were the Student's t-statistic and Pearson's product-moment correlation (r.). One additional type of analysis was undertaken in which the aggregate student achievement scores of the two groups were numerically compared with those of New York State's reference norm.

1. Student's t-Statistic—Testing for Research Question #1
   Under normal circumstances (i.e., when working with samples that have known variances), the z-statistic would be used in determining the mean differences of the two samples or populations. But because the student achievement indicator data were derived from independent samples with unknown variances, coupled with the fact that, at least in the district subcategories, some of the data pairs had less than 30 variables, the Student's t-statistic was used instead (see Johnson, 1992). (Note: 30 is the statistical threshold for treating samples as either large or small.) In all instances in which t-tests were performed, the objective was to see whether there are significant differences in the academic performance indicators of the professional and political school boards. As a way to further test suggestions in the literature review that professional boards would likely perform higher than political boards, two-tailed t-tests were performed at the .05 alpha level on all four areas of student achievement (graduation/college rates, Pupil Evaluation Program, Program Evaluation Test, Regents Examinations). Altogether, a total of 49 student achievement indicators were used in the various comparisons.

a. *Comparing the educational performance of the professional and political districts.*

The first research question called for mean difference tests using various sample sizes to see if there are statistically significant differences between the aggregate performance indicators of the professional and political districts. Table 5 below operationalizes this research objective by comparing the student achievement indicators of the two groups, using the t-test for mean difference statistic at the alpha level of .05. The table summarizes the research design, which includes the dependent and independent variables as well as the type of statistical analysis to be applied.

Table 5

Design for testing research question #1: T-test for comparing the educational performance of the professional and political districts

Research Question #1	Independent Variable	Dependent Variable	Analysis
1) Do the aggregated means of the student achievement indicators differ?	1) Professional style	1) Graduation rates/percent to college	T-test for mean difference (sample-mean to sample-mean)
	2) Political style	2) PEP	
		3) PET	
		4) Regents Examinations	

The research design presented in Table 5 called for a specific testing process and procedure as follows:

Step 1:

A running list of the districts that responded to the survey was maintained up to 3 months past the response deadline for returning the completed surveys. The extra time was necessary to accommodate late returns.

Step 2:

The style classification task was subsequently undertaken, whereby the surveys were first put through a screening test using Greene's (1992) "two-out-of-three" formula. Specifically, districts were classified as "professional" if the board president gave at least two of the following "professional" responses: spent less than 3 hours per week responding to parents, received more than 90% unanimous decisions, and completely maintained the distinction between policy making and administration. Conversely, a board was classified as "political" if the president gave at least two of the following "political" responses: spent more than 3 hours per week responding to parents, experienced less than 90% unanimous decisions, and exhibited nonrecognition of the distinction between policy making and administration (Greene, 1992, p. 224). (Note: The professional and political coding constituted the independent variables.)

Step 3:

With the list of respondents now in place, NYSED's electronic database on district performance was electronically imported into a personal computer to identify and extract the names and performance data of the responding districts.

Step 4:

From this electronic master list, additional sorting was performed and the results were stored in separate files as follows:

a) A statewide pool of **professional** districts
b) A statewide pool of **political** districts

c) An urban pool of **professional** districts
d) An urban pool of **political** districts

e) A suburban pool of **professional** districts
f) A suburban pool of **political** districts

g) A rural pool of **professional** districts
h) A rural pool of **political** districts

Step 5:

Each list was, in turn, reformatted so that the "total" and "pooled average" of every performance indicator for each group could be obtained. The resulting pooled averages for each of the policy-making styles are shown in Tables 11 A-B (statewide), 12 A-B (urban), 13 A-B (suburban), and 14 A-B (rural), respectively by district type.

Step 6:

The resulting set of pooled aggregate data for the two styles were, in turn, compared along the indicators of the four major subject areas (graduation/percent to college, PEP, PET, and Regents Examinations) to see if they differ from each other and by how much. The tests were conducted with the Student's t-test statistic at the .05 level of significance.

b. *Comparing the educational performance of the professional and political districts with the state's averages.*

   The second research question called for a numerical comparison of the aggregate performance indicators of the two groups with the New York State averages. The idea was to see if there are simple numerical differences between the three groups as well as how each group fares relative to the New York State's averages. Table 6 operationalizes this research objective by comparing the aggregate student achievement indicators of the professional and political districts with those of the New York State reference norm. The table summarizes the research design that includes the dependent and independent variables as well as the type of statistical analysis to be applied.

Table 6

Design for testing research question #2: T-test for comparing the educational performance of the professional and political districts, with the state averages

Research Question #2	Independent Variable	Dependent Variable	Analysis
1) Do the aggregated means of the student achievement indicators differ?	1) Professional style	1) Graduation rates/ percent to college	A numerical comparison of the professional and political indicators against NYS norm/average
	2) Political style	2) PEP	
	3) New York State averages	3) PET	
		4) Regents Exam	

The design for research question # 2, presented in Table 6, called for the same type of data manipulation steps as the one carried out for research question #1 (steps 1-5) in Table 5 above, but it goes one step further to compare the statewide average performance data with the corresponding indicators of the professional and political indicators to see where each group's scores fall relative to the state average. The outcome of this comparison is shown in Tables 14 A-B, 15 A-B, and 16 A-B in the Results and Findings section.

2. Pearson's Product-Moment Correlation "r"—Testing for Research Question #3
   In order to determine whether there are possible relationships between the socioeconomic status of school districts and policy-making style, the Pearson's product-moment "r" correlation test was performed. This was a targeted effort to find out whether a district's SES is a factor in determining a board's policy-making style, which would ultimately imply such a role (by poverty) in the educational performance of the districts. The subject of poverty and its potential impact on educational performance is also discussed in some detail in chapter VII. Table 7 below operationalizes this research objective by testing for the correlation coefficient of policy-making style and district SES. The table summarizes the research design, which includes the dependent and independent variables and the type of statistical analysis to be applied.

Table 7

Design for testing research question #3: Pearson's product-moment correlation coefficient "r" for testing the relationship between policy-making style and district SES

Research Question #3	Independent Variable	Dependent Variable	Analysis
1) Is there a relationship between district SES (as measured by CPI) and a board's policy-making style?	Census Poverty Index (CPI)	Policy-making style	Pearson's product-moment "r" correlation

The research design presented in Table 7 also called for the same type of data manipulation steps as the one carried out for research question #1 (steps 1-4) in Table 5 above, but it goes two steps further as follows:

Step 5:

The values that were used in performing the statistical operation for correlation coefficient were obtained from the survey data as follows: (1) the total count of respondents, (2) the coded values for policy-making style (i.e., the X values), and (3) the coded values from NYSED's Census Poverty Index (i.e., the Y values).

Step 6:

The values were, in turn, used to perform the statistical test for the correlation coefficient.

<u>CHAPTER XIII</u>

Results and Findings

The preceding chapter described the various steps that were followed in conducting this study as follows: (1) the random and stratified selection of the samples, (2) the classification of the districts according to their policy-making style, and (3) the comparison of their aggregate educational performance indicators. In this chapter, the outcomes of the statistical analyses are presented in such a way that the outcomes in the statewide sample come first, followed by those of the various district categories:

A. Survey response rates.

The survey response rates for the statewide and district level outcomes are presented below as follows:

1. Statewide outcomes

Of the 258 school board presidents who were surveyed, 159 responded, yielding a response rate of 61.6%. Of the 159 responses that were received, 39, or 24.5%, were from urban districts; 62, or 39.0%, were from suburban districts; and 58, or 36.5%, were from rural districts. Once again, with regard to the relative strength of the generalizability of the outcomes to larger populations, the urban category is highest with 67.4%, followed by the rural district with 29%, and lastly by the suburban districts with 14%.

2. ***Outcomes by district type***

   Among the three district categories, the response rate was highest in the urban category, followed by the suburban and, finally, the rural. Specifically, of the 58 urban board presidents surveyed, 39, or 67.2%, of them responded. In the suburban category, 100 board presidents were surveyed, and 62 of them responded, which represents a response rate of 62.0%. Finally, in the rural category, 100 were surveyed and 58, or 58.0%, of them responded. Table 8 below contains information on the number and percent of responses (i.e., response rates) within the various district categories, broken down by type of district.

Table 8
Response rate data (number/percent) broken down by district type

District Category	Number of Respondents	% of Respondents	% of Respondents Relative to Population
Urban Districts	39	67.2	67.4%
Suburban Districts	62	62.0	14.0%
Rural Districts	58	58.0	29.0%
Total	**159**	**61.6**	**22.5%**

3. ***Summary of observations***

   Given that most board members work elsewhere and, as such, are seldom on district grounds during normal business hours, the overall response rate of 61.6%, and individual district rates of 67%, 62%, and 58% in the urban, suburban, and rural districts, respectively, are thought to be sufficiently high. It took persistence, perseverance, and a lot of time and money to get the response rate to this level. It should be noted that this "structural unavailability" of school board members during normal business hours would be especially problematic for researchers who employ qualitative research methods such as personal interviews, field observations, or other kinds of follow-up tasks.

Finally, it is worth noting here as well that a total of 128, or 80.5%, of the respondents asked to receive copies of the study findings upon the completion of the study. This number is unusually high, but is not altogether surprising given that the subject matter is of great interest to school board members, superintendents, parents, and the community at large.

B. Grouping school districts by policy-making style.

In order to determine the policy-making style of the boards in the various districts, the surveys were put through a screening test using Greene's (1992) "two-out-of-three" screening formula. Specifically, districts were classified as "professional" if the board president gave at least two of the following "professional" responses: spent less than 3 hours per week responding to parents, experienced more than 90% unanimous decisions, and completely maintained the distinction between policy making and administration. Conversely, a board was classified as "political" if the president gave at least two of the following "political" responses: spent more than 3 hours per week responding to parents, experienced less than 90% unanimous decisions, and exhibited nonrecognition of the distinction between policy making and administration (Greene, 1992, p. 224). Table 9 below shows precisely how the policy-making style of school boards were classified as either "professional" or "political" using the survey responses of their board presidents.

Table 9

Classification of the policy-making style of school boards as either "professional" or "political" based on the survey responses of their board presidents

	Less than 3 hours per week responding to parents and groups?	More than 90% unanimous decisions by the board	Complete distinction between policy making style and administra-tion	# of Responses	Type	District Type Urban	 Suburban	 Rural
1	Yes	Yes	Yes	40	Prof.	9	13	18
2	Yes	Yes	No	25	Prof.	5	9	11
3	Yes	No	Yes	11	Prof.	1	7	3
4	No	Yes	Yes	22	Prof.	3	13	6
5	Yes	Blank	Yes	1	Prof.	0	0	1
6	Blank	Yes	Yes	1	Prof.	0	1	0
			Sub-Total	**100**		**18**	**43**	**39**
7	No	No	No	19	Pol.	9	7	3
8	No	No	Yes	4	Pol.	0	3	1
9	No	Yes	No	20	Pol.	6	7	7
10	Yes	No	No	15	Pol.	5	2	8
11	No	No	Blank	1	Pol.	1		
			Subtotal	**59**		**21**	**19**	**19**
			GRAND TOTAL	**159**		**39**	**62**	**58**

1. ***Statewide outcomes***

   As Tables 9 and 10 show, the screening process yielded two different groups: "professional" and "political," which constituted the two experimental treatment conditions or independent variables. Specifically, of the 159 districts that responded, 100, or 63%, of them were classified as "professional," having indicated in their survey that their board (1) spends less than 3 hours per week responding to parents, (2) makes more than 90% unanimous decisions, and (3) completely maintains the distinction between policy making and administration. The remaining 59, or 37%, districts were classified as "political" upon indicating that their board: (1) spends more than 3 hours per week responding to parents, (2) makes less than 90% unanimous decisions, and (3) does not recognize or follow the distinction between policy making and administration.

2. ***Outcomes by district type***

   The style splits in the various district types were slightly different, particularly in the urban category, which had a reverse outcome compared to the others. (Also see Tables 9 and 10 for the outcome of the response pattern within district categories). Of the 39 districts in this category, 18, or 46%, were classified as professional, while 21, or 54%, were classified as political. The suburban and rural districts, on the other hand, mirrored the statewide outcome by having more of their districts in the professional category. Of the 62 districts in the suburban category, 43, or 69%, were classified as professional, while 19, or 31%, were classified as political. And in the rural district category,

39, or 67%, were classified as professional, and 19, or 33%, were classified as political. See Table 10 below for a breakdown of the style classification information by district type. It shows the number of respondents from each district category (urban, suburban, and rural) and how each of them is split in terms of policy-making style.

Table 10

The classification of the urban, suburban, and rural district respondents according to their policy-making style using Greene's (1992) two-out-of-three formula

		Classified as Professional		Classified as Political	
District Category	Total # of Respondents	#	%	#	%
Urban Districts	39	18	46%	21	54%
Suburban Districts	62	43	69%	19	31%
Rural Districts	58	39	67%	19	33%
Total	**159**	**100**	**63%**	**59**	**37%**

Note: Includes information on four of the Big 5 districts; New York City is excluded

3. *Summary of observations*

As indicated above, the classification process showed that 63% of the school districts in the study have a professional policy-making style, while the remaining 37% have a political style. It should be noted that this 63% to 37% split in the statewide outcome mirrored the outcome of the New Jersey study conducted by Greene (1992) in which he found a 61% to 39% split between professional and political boards, respectively.

In the individual district categories, the response rates were generally high, with the urban category being the highest. This high response in the urban category was not altogether surprising, given that nearly all of the eligible districts in that category were surveyed. On the other hand, the response rate in the suburban category can be said to be surprisingly high, given that there was somewhat of an underrepresentation in the survey pool relative to the number of such districts in the state. The rural category registered the lowest response rate despite its sizeable representation in the survey pool. This seemed surprising at first, but follow-up telephone calls later showed that rural board presidents tend to be more reluctant and generally guarded about responding to surveys.

C. Answering research question #1—a comparison of the student achievement indicators of the professional and political districts.

The comparisons on student achievement were performed in four areas used by the New York State Education Department in assessing district performance. They include graduation/college rates, Pupil Evaluation Program, Program Evaluation Tests, and Regents Examinations. The following is a description of the observations made in the statewide sample as well as within the three district categories.

1. Observations: Statewide sample (63% professional; 37% political)

This was a comparison of all the districts in the statewide sample (N=159), including four of the Big 5 districts in the urban category (i.e., Buffalo, Rochester, Syracuse, and Yonkers; New York City was excluded from the study because of its unique configuration as well as its extraordinarily large student population).

The t-test analyses showed that the student achievement indicators of the professional districts were slightly higher than those of the political districts in 8 out of 49 (or 16.3%) indicators; the observed differences in these indicators were statistically significant at the .05 level. This gap in performance occurred mostly in the Regents Examinations component as follows: 2 items in Sequential Math, 2 items in Sequential Math 2, 3 items in Earth Science, and 1 item in Physics. The summary data on the student achievement indicators for the professional and political districts on the Core assessment areas and Regents Examinations components are shown in Tables 11-A and 11-B, respectively. The tables compare the performance indicators of the professional and political districts (i.e., the two columns on the right) using the performance indicators displayed in the left column. It is worth pointing out that in addition to the 8 indicators that showed statistically significant differences, 37 (or 75.5%) other professional indicators also tended to be generally higher than those of the political districts, as indicated by the brackets.

Table 11-A

The comparison of the aggregate performance indicators of the professional and political districts on the Core academic assessment areas using a two-sample, two-tailed t-test—statewide sample

Performance Indicators		Prof. N=100 Mean (%)	Pol. N=59 Mean (%)
A.	**Graduation and Percent to College Rate**		
1)	Percent of Regents Diplomas (1988/89)	38.6	[39.7]
2)	Percent of Regents Diplomas (1996/97)	[47.2]	44.3
3)	Percent of 1995/96 to college	[76.8]	75.7
B.	**Pupil Evaluation Program**		
4)	Grade 3 Reading	90.8	[91.1]
5)	Grade 3 Math	[98.7]	98.1
6)	Grade 5 Writing	[92.1]	90.4
7)	Grade 6 Reading	[93.5]	92.6
8)	Grade 6 Math	[97.5]	96.2
C.	**Program Evaluation Tests**		
9)	Grade 4 Sci. Obi. Test (Content)	[23.3]	22.6
10)	Grade 4 Sci. Obj. Test (Skills)	[12.7]	12.3
11)	Grade 4 Sd. (Manipulative Skills)	[33.8]	33.4
12)	Grade 6 Social Studies	44.4	[44.6]
13)	Grade 8 Social Studies	[47.7]	46.9

[ ] = Indicates higher numerical value

* = Indicates statistically significant difference between the two sample means

Table 11-B

The comparison of the aggregate performance indicators of the professional and political districts on the Regents Examinations component using a two-sample, two-tailed t-test-statewide sample

Performance Indicators			Prof. N=100 Mean (%)	Pol. N=59 Mean (%)
Comprehensive English	14)	% of A.G.E. tested	[72.8]	70.1
	15)	% of tested passing	[82.7]	81.9
	16)	% of A.G.E. passing	[64.3]	60.4
Global Studies	17)	% of A.G.E. tested	[75.7]	72.3
	18)	% of tested passing	[68.4]	66.8
	19)	% of A.G.E. passing	[55.4]	51.5
U.S. History/Government	20)	% of A.G.E. tested	[69.2]	67.8
	21)	% of tested passing	[75.7]	73.9
	22)	% of A.G.E. passing	[54.4]	51.8
Comprehensive French	23)	% of A.G.E. tested	[16.3]	16.0
	24)	% of tested passing	76.7	[84.3]
	25)	% of A.G.E. passing	[15.3]	15.4
Comprehensive Spanish	26)	% of A.G.E. tested	[34.1]	31.9
	27)	% of tested passing	[87.9]	85.1
	28)	% of A.G.E passing	[32.4]	29.8
Sequential Math 1	29)	% of A.G.E. tested	[89.5]	82.6
	30)	% of tested passing	[77.7]*	69.7*
	31)	% of A.G.E. passing	[71.0]*	61.7*
Sequential Math 2	32)	% of A.G.E. tested	[71.0]*	61.4*
	33)	% of tested passing	[73.2]	67.7
	34)	% of A.G.E. passing	[54.3]*	44.7*
Sequential Math 3	35)	% of A.G.E. tested	[49.1]	45.7
	36)	% of tested passing	[81.6]	78.3
	37)	% of A.G.E. passing	[41.9]	38.2
Earth Science-94 ED	38)	% of A.G.E. tested	[48.2]*	28.7*
	39)	% of tested passing	[54.3]*	39.3*
	40)	% of A.G.E. passing	[38.4]*	22.4*
Biology	41)	% of A.G. E. tested	[67.0]	63.2
	42)	% of tested passing	[76.5]	73.7
	43)	% of A.G.E. passing	[57.6]	50.8
Chemistry	44)	% of A.G.E. tested	[45.5]	42.1
	45)	% of tested passing	[79.2]	78.0
	46)	% of A.G.E. passing	[39.3]	35.0
Physics	47)	% of A.G.E. tested	[26.2]	22.6
	48)	% of tested passing	[80.4]	80.1
	49)	% of A.G.E. passing	[23.5]	19.4*

[ ] = Indicates higher numerical value

* = Indicates statistically significant difference between the two sample means

A.G.E = Average Grade Enrollment

In an effort to find out how much of the observed differences might be attributable to the influence of the Big 4 districts, the same analysis was repeated without the Big 4 districts (*N*=155). But the outcome remained basically the same; the indicators for the professional districts were still higher than those of the political districts but this time by 7 out of 49 (or 14.3%) of the total number of indicators. This means that the potential influence of the Big 4 districts in the urban category was negligible. The differences were still confined to the Regents Examinations component.

2. Observations: Urban district sample (46% professional; 54% political)

The comparison in this category (*N*=39), revealed an even stronger showing by the professional group over the political group. Here, the student achievement indicators of the professional districts were higher than those of the political districts in 10 out of 49 (or 20.4%) of the total number of indicators. As was the case in the statewide sample, the differences occurred exclusively in the Regents Examinations component (English, Global Studies, Sequential Math 1, Sequential Math 3, Each Science, Biology, and Chemistry). Tables 12-A and 12-B contain summaries of the performance by the two groups of urban districts on the Core assessment areas and Regents Examinations components, respectively. The tables compare the performance indicators of the professional and political districts (i.e., the two columns on the right) using the performance indicators displayed in the left column. As with the case in the statewide sample, this table also shows that in addition to the 10 indicators that showed statistically significant differences, 36 (or 73.5%) other professional indicators also tended to be generally higher than those of the political districts, as indicated by the brackets.

Table 12-A

The comparison of the aggregate performance indicators of the professional and political districts on the Core academic assessment areas using a two-sample, two-tailed t-test-urban sample

Performance Indicators		Prof. N=18 Mean (%)	Pol. N=21 Mean (%)
A.	Graduation and Percent to College Rate		
	1) Percent of Regents Diplomas (1988/89)	[37.6]	32.8
	2) Percent of Regents Diplomas (1996/97)	[45.4]	41.4
	3) Percent of 1995/96 to college	[77.6]	76.2
B.	Pupil Evaluation Program		
	4) Grade 3 Reading	[92.3]	90.9
	5) Grade 3 Math	99.4	99.4
	6) Grade 5 Writing	86.9	[92.0]
	7) Grade 6 Reading	[93.2]	90.9
	8) Grade 6 Math	[97.4]	96.3
C.	Program Evaluation Tests		
	9) Grade 4 Sci. Obj. Test (Content)	[23.1]	20.9
	10) Grade 4 Sci. Obj. Test (Skills)	[12.6]	11.4
	11) Grade 4 Sci. (Manipulative Skills)	[34.0]	31.5
	12) Grade 6 Social Studies	[42.5]	41.1
	13) Grade 8 Social Studies	[47.6]	43.9

[ ] = Indicates higher numerical value
* = Indicates statistically significant difference between the two sample means

Table 12-B

The comparison of the aggregate performance indicators of the professional and political districts on the Regents Examinations component using a two-sample, two-tailed t-test—urban sample

Performance Indicators			Prof. N=18 Mean (%)	Pol. N=21 Mean (%)
Comprehensive English	14)	% of A.G.E. tested	[67.3]	59.1
	15)	% of tested passing	[90.8]*	80.7*
	16)	% of A.G.E. passing	[60.8]	50.5
Global Studies	17)	% of A.G.E. tested	[68.7]	57.6
	18)	% of tested passing	[77.8]*	64.8*
	19)	% of A.G.E. passing	[53.5]	41.3*
U.S. History/Government	20)	% of A.G.E. tested	[62.7]	57.4
	21)	% of tested passing	[82.6]	76.0
	22)	% of A.G.E. passing	[51.8]	44.0
Comprehensive French	23)	% of A.G.E. tested	[14.9]	14.7
	24)	% of tested passing	90.2	[93.3]
	25)	% of A.G.E. passing	[14.2]	14.1
Comprehensive Spanish	26)	% of A.G.E. tested	[31.4]	31.0
	27)	% of tested passing	[92.9]	91.2
	28)	% of A.G.E. passing	[29.3]	28.5
Sequential Math 1	29)	% of A.G.E. tested	[88.2]	77.9
	30)	% of tested passing	[77.0]	70.7
	31)	% of A.G.E. passing	[68.2]	56.2
Sequential Math 2	32)	% of A.G.E. tested	[65.7]	54.8*
	33)	% of tested passing	[76.1]	69.0
	34)	% of A.G.E. passing	[50.8]*	38.7*
Sequential Math 3	35)	% of A.G.E. tested	[44.3]*	39.5*
	36)	% of tested passing	[85.7]*	77.7*
	37)	% of A.G.E. passing	[38.3]	31.6
Earth Science-94 ED	38)	% of A.G.E. tested	[23.9]	19.9
	39)	% of tested passing	[42.6]	39.9
	40)	% of A.G.E. passing	[20.3]*	14.3*
Biology	41)	% of A.G.E. tested	[56.6]	56.3
	42)	% of tested passing	[79.0]	67.0
	43)	% of A.G.E. passing	[48.1]*	42.2*
Chemistry	44)	% of A.G.E. tested	[44.8]*	36.9*
	45)	% of tested passing	[82.7]	78.0
	46)	% of A.G.E. passing	[37.5]	29.8
Physics	47)	% of A.G.E. tested	[24.7]	21.7
	48)	% of tested passing	[86.6]	82.9
	49)	% of A.G.E. passing	[22.1]	18.2

[ ] = Indicates higher numerical value
* = Indicates statistically significant difference between the two sample means
A.G.E. = Average Grade Enrollment

3. Observations: Suburban sample (69% professional; 31% political)

The performance comparison in this category (*N*=62) did not reveal any statistically significant differences between the professional and political districts. See Tables 13-A and 13-B for the summary tables showing the comparative performance of the two groups on the Core assessment areas and Regents Examinations components, respectively. The tables compare the performance indicators of the professional and political districts (i.e., the two columns on the right) using the performance indicators displayed in the left column.

Table 13-A

The comparison of the aggregate performance indicators of the professional and political districts on the Core academic assessment areas using a two-sample, two-tailed t-test-suburban sample

Performance Indicators			Prof. N=18	Pol. N=21
A.	**Graduation and Percent to College Rates**			
	1)	Percent of Regents Diplomas (1988/89)	42.2	[49.5]
	2)	Percent of Regents Diplomas (1996/97)	[50.5]	49.0
	3)	Percent of 1995/96 to college	[82.5]	79.1
B.	**Pupil Evaluation Program**			
	4)	Grade 3 Reading	88.3	[94.5]
	5)	Grade 3 Math	97.4	[99.9]
	6)	Grade 5 Writing	91.3	[97.0]
	7)	Grade 6 Reading	91.9	[97.6]
	8)	Grade 6 Math	96.5	[99.2]
C.	**Program Evaluation Tests**			
	9)	Grade 4 Sci. Obj. Test (Content)	23.3	[23.5]
	10)	Grade 4 Sci. Obj. Test (Skills)	12.7	[12.8]
	11)	Grade 4 Sci. (Manipulative Skills)	33.4	[34.5]
	12)	Grade 6 Social Studies	44.2	[47.9]
	13)	Grade 8 Social Studies	46.0	[49.5]

[ ] = Indicates higher numerical value
* = Indicates statistically significant difference between the two sample means

Table 13-B

The comparison of the aggregate performance indicators of the professional and political districts on the Regents Examinations using a two-sample, two-tailed t-test—suburban sample

Performance Indicators			Prof. N=43 Mean (%)	Pol. N=19 Mean (%)
Comp. English	14)	% of A.G.E. tested	72.6	[79.0]
	15)	% of tested passing	76.7	[82.8]
	16)	% of A.G.E. passing	64.6	[69.0]
Global Studies	17)	% of A.G.E. tested	73.6	[83.5]
	18)	% of tested passing	67.6	[69.1]
	19)	% of A.G.E. passing	57.5	[59.9]
U.S. History/Gov't	20)	% of A.G.E. tested	68.6	[75.1]
	21)	% of tested passing	[71.8]	71.1
	22)	% of A.G.E. passing	55.2	[56.6]
Comp. French	23)	% of A.G.E. tested	[15.3]	14.5
	24)	% of tested passing	[80.7]	77.1
	25)	% of A.G.E. passing	[14.9]	14.1
Comp. Spanish	26)	% of A.G.E. tested	38.4	[39.2]
	27)	% of tested passing	85.8	[89.6]
	28)	% of A.G.E. passing	36.5	[37.3]
Sequential Math 1	29)	% of A.G.E. tested	85.6	[86.5]
	30)	% of tested passing	[76.3]	70.9
	31)	% of A.G.E. passing	[69.6]	68.2
Sequential Math 2	32)	% of A.G.E. tested	[73.1]	67.9
	33)	% of tested passing	[69.7]	68.2
	34)	% of A.G.E. passing	[56.3]	51.2
Sequential Math 3	35)	% of A.G.E. tested	[53.2]	51.3
	36)	% of tested passing	[77.8]	75.5
	37)	% of A.G.E. passing	[45.9]	43.4
Earth Science94 ED	38)	% of A.G.E. tested	[43.0]	41.8
	39)	% of tested passing	52.2	[54.8]
	40)	% of A.G.E. passing	[35.6]	35.4
Biology	41)	% of A.G.E. tested	[69.3]	66.5
	42)	% of tested passing	72.5	[77.4]
	43)	% of A.G.E. passing	[60.0]	57.5
Chemistry	44)	% of A.G.E. tested	[49.3]	48.7
	45)	% of tested passing	[77.6]	77.1
	46)	% of A.G.E. passing	[43.6]	42.0
Physics	47)	% of A.G.E. tested	[29.7]	25.4
	48)	% of tested passing	78.3	78.3
	49)	% of A.G.E. passing	[26.5]	22.1

[ ] = Indicates higher numerical value
* = Indicates statistically significant difference between the two sample means
A.G.E. = Average Grade Enrollment

4. Observations: Rural sample (67% professional; 33% political)

In this final level of comparison (*N*=58), the student achievement indicators of the professional districts were also higher than those of the political districts in 7 out of 49 (or 14.3%) of the total number of indicators. As was the case with the statewide and urban districts, the differences occurred in two assessment areas: 1 item in the PEP category (5th Grade Writing) and 6 items in the Regents Examinations component (Sequential Math 1, Sequential Math 2, and Earth Sciences). Tables 14-A and 14-B contain summaries of the performance by the two groups of school districts on the Core assessment areas and Regents Examinations components, respectively. The tables compare the performance indicators of the professional and political districts (i.e., the two columns on the right) using the performance indicators displayed in the left column. This table also shows that in addition to the 7 indicators that showed statistically significant differences, 36 (or 73.5%) other professional indicators also tended to be generally higher than those of the political districts, as indicated by the brackets.

Table 14-A

The comparison of the aggregate performance indicators of the professional and political districts on the Core academic assessment areas using a two-sample, two-tailed t-test-rural sample performance indicators

Performance Indicators			Prof. N=39 Mean (%)	Pol. N=19 Mean (%)
A.	Graduation and percent to college rates			
	1)	Percent of Regents Diplomas (1988/89)	35.5	[38.0]
	2)	Percent of Regents Diplomas (1996/97)	[44.4]	42.6
	3)	Percent of 1995/96 to college	70.7	[71.7]
B.	Pupil Evaluation Program			
	4)	Grade 3 Reading	[93.0]	88.1
	5)	Grade 3 Math	[99.7]	94.7
	6)	Grade 5 Writing	[95.3]*	81.9*
	7)	Grade 6 Reading	[95.4]	89.6
	8)	Grade 6 Math	[98.6]	93.3
C.	Program Evaluation Tests			
	9)	Grade 4 Sci. Obj. Test (Content)	23.5	23.5
	10)	Grade 4 Sci. Obj. Test (Skills)	12.6	[12.7]
	11)	Grade 4 Sci. (Manipulative Skills)	34.2	[34.5]
	12)	Grade 6 Social Studies	[45.5]	45.1
	13)	Grade 8 Social Studies	[49.6]	47.5]

[ ] = Indicates higher numerical value

* = Indicates statistically significant difference between the two sample means

Table 14-B

The comparison of the aggregate performance indicators of the professional and political districts on the Regents Examinations component using a two-sample, two-tailed t-test-rural sample

Performance Indicators			Prof. N=39 Mean (%)	Pol. N=I9 Mean (%)
Comp. English	14)	%of A.G.E. tested	[75.6]	73.4
	15)	% of tested passing	[85.4]	82.4
	16)	% of A.G.E. passing	[65.5]	62.9
Global Studies	17)	% of A.G.E. tested	[81.3]	77.3
	18)	% of tested passing	64.9	[66.6]
	19)	% of A.G.E. passing	54.1	[54.3]
U.S. History/Gov't	20)	% of A.G.E. tested	[72.8]	72.0
	21)	% of tested passing	[76.9]	74.3
	22)	% of A.G.E. passing	54.6	[55.5]
Comp. French	23)	% of A.G.E. tested	18.1	[18.9]
	24)	% of tested passing	66.1	[81.6]
	25)	% of A.G.E. passing	17.3	[18.3]
Comp. Spanish	26)	% of A.G.E. tested	[30.6]	25.5
	27)	% of tested passing	[88.0]	73.8
	28)	% of A.G.E. passing	29.2	23.9
Sequential Math 1	29)	% of A.G.E. tested	[94.3]	83.8
	30)	% of tested passing	[79.7]*	67.4*
	31)	% of A.G.E. passing	[74.0]	61.4*
Sequential Math 2	32)	% of A.G.E. tested	[71.1]	62.2
	33)	% of tested passing	[75.7]*	65.9*
	34)	% of A.G.E. passing	[53.6]	44.9
Sequential Math 3	35)	% of A.G.E. tested	[47.0]	46.8
	36)	% of tested passing	[83.7]	81.6
	37)	% of A.G.E. passing	39.2	[40.4]
Earth Science94 ED	38)	% of A.G.E. tested	[65.2]*	25.3*
	39)	% of tested passing	[62.1]*	30.8*
	40)	% of A.G.E. passing	[49.8]	18.3*
Biology	41)	% of A.G.E. tested	[69.3]	67.6
	42)	% of tested passing	[79.7]	77.3
	43)	% of A.G.E. passing	[59.3]	53.7
Chemistry	44)	% of A.G.E. tested	[41.7]	41.1
	45)	% of tested passing	[79.3]	79.0
	46)	% of A.G.E. passing	[35.4]	33.7
Physics	47)	% of A.G.E. tested	[22.9]	20.7
	48)	% of tested passing	[79.8]	78.9
	49)	% of A.G.E. passing	[20.8]	18.1

[ ] = Indicates higher numerical value
* = Indicates statistically significant difference between the two sample means
A.G.E. = Average Grade Enrollment

5. Summary of observations

The summary of observations made in the preceding section is presented below by district type.

a. **Statewide sample**—The comparisons above revealed small performance gains by the professional districts over the political districts, occurring exclusively in the Regents subject category. In addition to the statistically significant differences, several other professional indicators tended to be generally higher than those of the political indicators.

b. **Urban sample**—The pattern of outcomes in this category mirrored the statewide outcomes in the sense that the professional indicators were higher than those of the political boards. But they differed with respect to style split, with the political group outnumbering the professional here.

c. **Suburban sample**—The pattern of outcomes in the suburban category was different from the rest of the outcomes in the study in one important respect. Here, there was not a single statistically significant difference in the performance of the two groups. In fact, a simple numerical comparison of the indicators showed some performance gains by the political districts over the professional districts, which represents a reverse of the outcomes in the other comparisons. It would seem that this type of outcome directly challenges the suggestions in the literature review that appeared to ascribe poor performance to the political style and vice versa. It is unclear as to what extent the underrepresentation of this category in both the survey and study pool might be responsible for this type of outcome. But, if it proves to be valid, it would have more applicability to reality given that suburban districts represent more than half of the total number of districts in the state.

d. **Rural sample**—The pattern of outcomes in this category mirrored the statewide outcomes in all respects, including style splits and performance outcomes. But, one still has to wonder whether the board president's aversion to surveys could be problematic in any way.

D. Answering research question #2—observations of professional and political districts, as compared with New York State averages.

The outcomes discussed above involved a statistical comparison of the educational performance of the two groups. But, sometimes, performance is judged not only by the indicators but also by how they compare to the state's reference norms. This aspect of the analysis uses a simple numerical comparison to assess the performance of the districts relative to the New York State reference norms. In this additional analysis, the pooled performance indicators of the two groups were compared with those of New York State to see how consistent or different each group is to the state's average.

For instance, because the third grade reading indicator for the New York State is 86% in the 1998 School District Report Card, it will be curious to find out how or where each of the two groups fall relative to this reference indicator. If the suggestions in the literature review hold true, one would expect the professional indicators to be equal to or greater than the state's average, while those of the political group would be less than the state's average.

This turned out to be the general outcome of the comparison, although it was not entirely consistent in all the district categories or across all the subject areas. For instance, with the exception of suburban districts, the indicators of the professional group in the urban and rural samples were generally above the state's average, while those of the political group were below. The summary tables showing the comparative data are displayed and discussed below; they are presented in order by urban, suburban, and rural districts.

1. Comparison with New York State (urban sample)

Using a simple numerical comparison of the values with New York State averages, the results showed that more of the professional indicators were at or above the New York State reference figures and that a preponderance of the political indicators fell below them. See Table 15 below, which shows how the two groups of school districts fared relative to the state's average. The table presents a side-by-side comparison of the two groups on all subject areas. Specifically, it shows that 35 out of 48 (or 72.9%) of the pooled student achievement indicators for the professional districts were higher than the state's average. But only 9 out of 48 (or 18.8%) of the pooled student achievement indicators for the political districts were above the state's average. The higher performance (shown as number of indicators) by the professional districts was consistent within the individual subject areas as well: (1) graduation/ percent to college rates: 2 professional and 0 political; (2) Pupil Evaluation Program: 4 professional and 4 political; (3) Program Evaluation Tests: 4 professional and 0 political; and finally, 4) Regents Examinations: 25 professional and 5 political.

Table 15

Measures of school success: a comparison of the professional and political district performances against the New York State reference norm-urban sample

A	Number of items "at/above" NYS average	Prof.	Pol.
1	Graduation and percent to college*	2	0
2	Pupil Evaluation Program	4	4
3	Program Evaluation Tests	4	0
4	Regents Examinations	25	5
	Total	**35**	**9**
	Percent	**72.9%**	**18.8%**

B	Number of items "below" NYS	Prof.	Pol.
1	Graduation and percent to college*	0	2
2	Pupil Evaluation Program	1	1
3	Program Evaluation Tests	1	5
4	Regents Examinations	11	31
	Total	**13**	**39**
	Percent	**27.1%**	**81.3%**

* = Graduation rate only; the percent to college indicator for NYS was unavailable for comparison

[ ] = Higher percentage value indicator

Note: The base for the "total" and "percent" is 48 because of the missing percent-to-college indicator; otherwise, the base would have been 49.

2. Comparison with New York State (suburban sample)

The comparison of the student achievement indicators of the suburban districts with New York State averages resulted in an entirely different pattern of outcomes than was the case in the urban sample: the figures for the political districts were slightly higher than those of the professional districts relative to the state averages. Specifically, 38 out of 48 (or 79.2%) of the pooled student achievement indicators for the political districts were higher than the state's average, while only 36 out of 48 (or 75.00/9) of the indicators for the professional districts were above the state's average. This outcome is consistent with all the nonconforming observations that have been made in the suburban category throughout the course of this analysis. See Table 16 to view how the two groups of school districts fared relative to the state's average indicators. The table presents a side-by-side comparison of the two groups on all the subject areas.

As Table 16 shows, there was very little difference in performance between the two groups in this comparison, but it is worth noting that both the professional and political groups performed better than the state's averages in general. With respect to the subject areas, the political group did slightly better in the PEP category, with 5 indicators versus 4 indicators for the professional group, and in the Regents Examinations category, with 27 indicators versus 26 indicators. Again, these are negligible differences that should not be overemphasized. The following is a breakdown of the performance outcomes (shown as number of indicators) within the various subject areas: (1) graduation/percent to college rates: 2 for professional and 2 for political; (2) Pupil Evaluation Program: 4 professional and 5 political; (3) Program Evaluation Tests: 4 professional and 4 political; and finally, 4) Regents Examinations: 26 professional and 27 political.

Table 16

Measures of school success: a comparison of the professional and political district performances against the New York State reference norm-suburban sample

A	Number of items "at/above" NYS average	Prof.	Pol.
1	Graduation and percent to college*	2	2
2	Pupil Evaluation Program	4	5
3	Program Evaluation Tests	4	4
4	Regents Examinations	26	27
	Total	**36**	**38**
	Percent	**75.0%**	**79.2%**

B	Number of items "below" NYS	Prof.	Pol.
1	Graduation and percent to college*	0	0
2	Pupil Evaluation Program	1	0
3	Program Evaluation Tests	1	1
4	Regents Examinations	10	9
	Total	**12**	**10**
	Percent	**25.0%**	**20.8%**

* = Graduation rate only; the percent to college indicator for NYS was unavailable for comparison

[ ] = Higher percentage value indicator

Note: The base for the "total" and "percent" is 48 because of the missing percent-to-college indicator; otherwise, the base would have been 49.

3. Comparison with New York State (rural sample)

As was the case in the urban district category, the comparison of the pooled student achievement indicators of the rural districts with New York State averages revealed a pattern of higher performance by the professional districts over the political districts. However, the gap between the two groups was not as wide as it was in the urban category. Specifically, 39 out of 48 (or 81.3%) of the student achievement indicators for the professional districts were higher than the state's average. On the other hand, only 29 out of 48 (or 60.4%) of the student achievement indicators for the political districts were above the state's average. This means that over 50% of both groups of districts performed better than the state's average, with about a 20.9% gap between them. See Table 17 to view how the two groups of school districts fared relative to the state's average. The table presents a side-by-side comparison of the two groups on all the subject areas.

It should also be noted that the performance advantage (shown as number of indicators) demonstrated by the professional districts was consistent within the individual subject areas as well: (1) graduation/percent to college rates: 2 professional and 2 political; (2) Pupil Evaluation Program: 5 professional and 2 political; (3) Program Evaluation Tests: 5 professional and 5 political; and finally, 4) Regents Examinations: 27 professional and 20 political.

Table 17

Measures of school success: a comparison of the professional and political district performances against the New York State reference norm-rural sample

A	Number of items "at/above" NYS average	Prof.	Pol.
1	Graduation and percent to college*	2	2
2	Pupil Evaluation Program	5	2
3	Program Evaluation Tests	5	5
4	Regents Examinations	27	20
	Total	**39**	**29**
	Percent	**81.3%**	**60.4%**

B	Number of items "below" NYS	Prof.	Pol.
1	Graduation and percent to college*	0	0
2	Pupil Evaluation Program	0	0
3	Program Evaluation Tests	0	1
4	Regents Examinations	9	9
	Total	**9**	**10**
	Percent	**18.8%**	**39.6%**

* = Graduation rate only; the percent to college indicator for NYS was unavailable for comparison

[ ] = Higher percentage value indicator

Note: The base for the "total" and "percent" is 48 because of the missing percent-to-college indicator; otherwise, the base would have been 49.

4. Summary of observations

The numerical comparison with New York State's reference norm showed how the two styles in the various district categories differed from the New York State averages, with the professional districts placing generally above the state norm and the political districts placing below it. Here too, the suburban district was the exception, with the political indicators being slightly higher than those of the professional ones.

E. Answering research question #3—the relationship between census poverty index and policy-making style (Pearson's Product-Moment "r" correlation).

As noted in the methodology section, it was deemed to be critically important that any observed differences in performance (or lack thereof) between the two policy-making styles be associated principally—if not exclusively—with the policy-making styles. And because poverty tends to be suspected in student achievement issues, the correlation analysis between style and poverty took on an added importance. Specifically, there was a targeted effort to find out whether a district's SES is a factor in determining a board's policy-making style, which would ultimately imply such a role (by poverty) in the educational performance of the districts. This effort recognizes that there are far too many intervening variables for anyone to be able to make this determination with certainty.

1. The correlation coefficient variables

In order to perform a correlation analysis, the standard formula for calculating the correlation coefficient between two variables was applied. The formula calls for the establishment of certain facts and figures (variables) from the survey data in order to calculate the correlation coefficient as follows: a. Policy-making style—The policy-making style of the districts were represented as professional (coded as "1") and political (coded as "2"). b. Census

Poverty Index—This index came from NYSED and refers to the number of children 5-17 years of age in families below the poverty level, as determined by the 1990 federal census, divided by the total number of children within the district boundaries who are 5-17 years of age (NYSED, 1998, p. vi). The statistical variables have been summarized below in Table 18-A.

Table 18-A

Data summary for the correlation coefficient computation

Respondents	X Style	Y CPI	$X-\bar{X}$	$Y-\bar{Y}$	(X-X) (Y-Y)	$(X-X)^2$	$(Y-Y)^2$
159	218	1958	X=1.4	Y=12.3	117.4	37.2	9390.3

2. Computation of the coefficient

In addition to presenting the variables of the correlation coefficient computation, the calculation procedure for the correlation coefficient statistic, using the applicable variables, is outlined in Table 18-B.

Table 18-B

Calculation Steps for the Correlation Coefficient Statistic

a. $117.4 / \sqrt{37.2}\ \sqrt{9390.3}$

   $\sqrt{37.2} = 6.1$

   $\sqrt{9390.3} = 96.9$

b. 117.4/6.1 x 96.9

   6.1 x 96.9 = 591.1

c. 117.4/591.1 = .199 (rounded .20)

The outcome of r = .20 shows a very small relationship between policy-making style and SES. A further calculation of the coefficient of determination of $.20^2$ yielded a percentage output of 0.04%, which means that only 4% of the variation in either SES or style may be predicted by knowing the value of the other measure, and vice versa.

3. Summary of observations

The correlation coefficient "r" = .199 (rounded to .20) and a coefficient of determination of "r^2" = 0.04% were indicative of a very low predictive value between board style and SES. It is important to stress, however, that there is no inference whatsoever from this outcome that SES does or does not impact educational performance. The correct interpretation is that the policy-making style of school boards is minimally influenced by SES.

F. General conclusions.

On the basis of the mixed results and findings from this study, the following conclusions were reached:

First, that there is a preponderance of professional boards in the state sample as a whole; specifically, in the suburban and rural district categories, but not in the urban category.

Second, that the indicators for professional districts were generally higher in the statewide, urban, and rural categories, but not in the suburban category.

Third, that the potential impact of SES on board style in this particular study was quite minimal, but its indirect impact on student achievement still bears watching.

G. Summary of all the findings.

A table that summarizes all the findings has been provided (see Table 19) below. This table brings together all the relevant information about how the study was conducted and breaks the information down by district category. The various pieces of information include sample pool and return rates, policy-making style splits, the results of the t-tests on the samples, the comparison of the two styles with the New York State reference data, and the results of the correlation analysis.

Table 19

Summary of all study findings, including data on sample pool, response rates, style classification, t-test results, comparison with New York State reference norm, and correlation of Consumer Price Index (CPI) with policy-making style, by district category.

Sample categories	Statewide	Urban	Suburban	Rural
Sample pool	258	58	100	100
Response pool	159 or 61.6%	39 or 67.2%	62 or 62.0%	58 or 58.0%
Style splits (Prof. vs. Pol.)	63%-37%	46%-54%	69%-31%	67%-33%
T-test results (Prof. vs. Pol.)	45 of 49 (or 91.8%)	46 of 49 (or 93.9%)	27 of 49 (or 55.1%)	43 of 49 (or 87.8%)
	(8=< 0.05 alpha)	(10=< 0.05 alpha)	(0=< 0.05 alpha)	(7=< 0.05 alpha)
Comparison with NYS # and % above/below SRP (Prof. vs. Pol.)	Above	Above	Above	Above
	42 or 86% vs. 29 or 59%	36 or 73% vs. 10 or 20%	38 or 78% vs. 40 or 82%	40 or 82% vs. 29 or 59%
	Below	Below	Below	Below
	7 or 14% vs. 20 or 41%	13 or 27% vs. 39 or 80%	11 or 22% vs. 9 or 18%	9 or 18% vs. 20 or 41%
Correlation of CPI & Style 0.05	r=0.1990 (r2 = 0.0396)	—	—	—

PART THREE

CHAPTER XIV

Limitations of the Study

This study was limited to some extent by certain situational and methodological factors discussed below:

1. *Classification issues*

As indicated above, one methodological issue in this study relates to the limitation of the classification method to clearly distinguish districts by how well they typify each policy-making style. Finding a way to further distinguish districts by style and then test for evidence of a differential impact is, therefore, a research imperative in future probes of this topic. Suggestions on how to further develop or improve upon classification methodology are discussed in the recommendations section under "suggestions for further study" (chapter VIII).

Another kind of a classification issue has to do with the overall response patterns. Specifically, although the classification split was higher for professional districts in this study, as well as in Greene's (1992), one cannot know for certain whether boards that are fraught with conflict are simply less likely to respond, and one is also not able to verify the veracity of the responses by the answering districts. Any of these likely scenarios could skew the classification split.

2. *Generalizability issues*

Being that this study utilized a statistical sampling methodology rather than study the entire population of school boards, it suffers in the same way that similar studies would with respect to their generalizability. However, as long as the manipulations are carried out in accordance with sound statistical principles and methodology, such studies should be valid.

Also, the fact that, as with Greene's (1992) study, it was conducted in one state is problematic in terms of generalizing the outcomes. But, as Greene correctly points out, conducting the study in one state where the education laws and the electoral system are the same has the advantage of increasing its validity.

3. *Timing issues*

Methodologically, one can wonder whether there might be a "disconnect" between the classification of current boards and using 2-year-old data (i.e., 1996/97 data that were released in February 1998) to assess the performance of the districts. Could this gap or delay compromise validity in any way? Considering the fact that board tenure generally runs longer than 2 years in their initial term of office and that the vast majority of them get reelected, it stands to reason that certain ingrained beliefs, philosophies, practices, and the social climate would endure for a very long time in the districts. In fact, it would be extremely rare to encounter a complete turnover of the board or the other key players in any given district. Therefore, a 2-year gap in measuring district performance based on the actions of a sitting board would still be valid; a gap longer than 5 years, however, would be methodologically unsound, especially because some turnover of board members and a change in educational philosophy may occur after this length of time.

4. *Potential problems with the student achievement indicators used by NYSED*

As noted in the literature review section of this study, the report card system was adopted/incorporated into this study simply because it is currently the only system in use by the NYSED. It was equally noted that the system is not without certain inherent flaws. For instance, while examining the Regents Examinations component of the assessment system, it was discovered that part of the suburban districts' superior performance over the rest of the district categories stems from the fact that they (i.e., the suburban districts) would invariably register more students for the various exams than would actually pass those exams. This meant that they would score high on the indicator that measures "percent tested" but low on the item that measures "percent tested passing," which, ultimately, would boost their performance on the last item, "percent of AGE passing."

For the sake of illustration, two fictitious districts are compared below. Urban District A, with 100 students, registered only 50 students they strongly believe are ready to take the Global Studies test. Suburban District B, with its own 100 students, enrolled 80 students, some of who are not quite ready for the test but could try. If only half of the test-takers from each group pass, the Regents point system would look something like this:

Table 20

An illustration of the quirks in the Regents testing

#	Indicators	District A (Urban)	District B (Suburban)
1	% of A.G.E. tested	50%	80%
2	% of tested passing	50%	50%
3	% of A.G.E. passing	25%	40%
	Total Points	**125%**	**170%**

Ideally, it would seem that the only valid measure of academic excellence would be the "percent tested passing," especially because it measures the ability of those who take and pass the exams. The other two items are simply a "numbers game" that would benefit only districts that know how it works. This is truly a quirk in the Regents assessment component and should be addressed by NYSED. Table 21 was designed to expose just how bogus and potentially manipulable the three Regents assessment are.

The table, for instance, shows that the suburban district category (and to some extent the rural district category) performed rather poorly on the "percent tested passing" indicator, which truly measures student achievement. To put it differently, if the number of students tested is high, but the number passing is low, it means that a high number of potentially unprepared students are being registered to take tests. Therefore, merely registering a large number of students for tests looks good on the state's report card, regardless of how many of the students actually pass. Therefore, designing the testing process such that the "percent tested passing" indicator gets weighted more than the other indicators might improve the system. The extent to which this study might be affected by this obscure quirk in the district report card system cannot be determined; it is certainly an area ripe for future investigation.

Table 21

A summary table showing the number of districts in each category (urban, suburban, and rural) that performed at or above the state average on the three Regents indicators

	Urban		Suburban		Rural	
Assessment Criteria	Prof.	Pol.	Prof.	Pol.	Prof.	Pol.
% of A.G.E. Tested	6	1	11	11	9	6
Total	**7 or 17.9%**		**[22] or 35.5%**		**15 or 25.9%**	
% of Tested Passing	9	3	3	4	7	5
Total	**[12] or 30.8%**		**7 or 11.3%**		**[12] or 20.7%**	
% of Passing of A.G.E.	10	1	11	11	9	6
Total	**11 or 28.2%**		**[24] or 38.7%**		**20 or 54.5%**	

[ ] = Indicates higher numerical value

5. *Financial issues*

Finally, financial constraints were equally a factor in conducting this study. If money were not an object, the entire population of school boards in New York State would have been included in the study, thus eliminating the limitations of the sampling methodology.

CHAPTER XV

Definition of Terms and Concepts

School District Governance: A categorical reference to the management and control of schools, public or private (Rada, 1988). Within this broad definition, lies a finer distinction between policy making and administration. The former is traditionally used in connection with school boards, while the latter is used in connection with superintendents. The extent to which the lines between these two areas of authority are clearly drawn or are respected by either party determines the degree of board-superintendent conflict.

Board Orientation: A term that refers to, as well as is used interchangeably with, the phrase "policy-making style." It was used extensively by Greene (1992) to characterize boards as having either a "professional" or "political" policy-making style.

School District Performance: This refers to the overall condition or standing of a given school district relative to other districts in the study pool. In the literature review, this was measured by certain selected academic performance measures *operationalized* into testable variables. Each indicator was selected following a review of the literature on school district performance measures. The indicators essentially describe what to look for in healthy, high-performing schools and school districts. Specifically, the indicators of school district performance include items that are referenced in the school board literature, which are also being used by the NYSED to assess school district performance.

CHAPTER XVI

Recommendations

(As contained in the original study/dissertation)

As indicated above, it is important to characterize this study and the new ground it covered on student achievement as exploratory and descriptive. It would, therefore, benefit from further research into its major concepts and methodology. However, based on the outcomes and some of the lessons learned from the study, a few recommendations have been put forward as follows.

1. Engage the NYSED to devise certain indicators, including the various style classification methods mentioned in the education literature. This would help in the monitoring and redirecting of the policy-making styles of school boards. This recommendation essentially recognizes the fact that the control of school districts is the ultimate responsibility of the state government, even though it is structurally delegated to local communities. If it turns out that a board's policy-making style impacts its educational performance in some fashion, it would behoove NYSED to become a key player in changing people's mindset and redirecting school boards toward adopting the style that works.

2. The NYSED is encouraged to continue on its current path of revising the district assessment system to make it fair,

equitable, and more meaningful. This recommendation recognizes some of the inherent flaws in the current assessment system and simply calls on the NYSED to continue its focus on the problem.

3. Rethink, revisit, and ultimately amend the New York State's education laws, which, at the time the study was conducted, was viewed as being quite vague and, therefore, partly responsible for the confusion on board-superintendent roles in New York State. A clearly defined set of roles and expectations for school boards and superintendents would help to reduce conflict and turf wars between the two key players.

Suggestions for Further Study

For anyone looking to replicate, improve upon, or simply use this study as part of a conceptual framework, a few suggestions are in order. Specifically, the prospective researcher should consider:

1. Modifying Greene's (1992) classification system slightly such that it can produce groupings of school districts not only by the two policy-making styles but also by how well each district typifies a given policy-making style—this is what I have called the "exemplar" system, which rates a district on a scale of 1 to 2 for each style on how well it typifies that particular style. This would yield such groupings as "professional 1 or 2" and "political 1 or 2," depending on how well those districts typify the policy-making style, with "1" being the best fit and

"2" being a loose fit. As noted above, the attempt was made in this study to compare the performance of an "all-professional" pool with that of an "all-political" pool, which yielded some interesting outcomes.

2. Doing a mix of quantitative and qualitative analysis with respect to classifying boards by their policy-making style. This would undoubtedly take a longer time to conduct and would cost more money but would yield additional useful information. Such an expanded study could entail doing surveys, interviews, and field observations as well as traveling and the use of certain monitoring equipment. The major benefit to this comprehensive approach would be to guard against the potential for board presidents to under—or overreport certain situations in the district, either purposely or due to a true lack of knowledge.

3. If resources allow, it may behoove the next researcher to also investigate the superintendent's role in the governance dynamics. It may be recalled that Katz (1993) theorized that district dynamics is a function of the right "match-up" between the board and the superintendent. The challenge here lies in operationalizing and quantifying the style of the superintendent so that it can be measured either qualitatively or quantitatively. This set of information and those that would be obtained from the school board would, in turn, be manipulated to measure their impact.

4. It might also be worthwhile to conduct this study in all 50 states, either through sampling or by a study of the

entire population. This would yield conclusions that are potentially generalizable to the nation as a whole. Furthermore, and as indicated above, it will show the various splits in terms of professional and political styles and, by so doing, reveal the various subject areas as well as part of the country where special attention may be needed.

5. It would be worthwhile to pay more attention to the suburban districts because of their unique performance outcomes in the study. This should include an initial examination of the unique characteristics of the suburban category (size, dominant policy-making style, board and superintendent tenure, income, gender, etc.) to better pin down the specific variable or group of variables that underlies their higher performance over the rest of the districts categories as well as the apparent absence of the impact of style on educational outcomes.

6. Recognizing the potential for distortion in the district assessment methodology, it might be worthwhile to conduct the academic performance analysis by separating out the three Regents criteria for an in-depth review. If this isolation approach changes the outcome of any such study substantially, then it would confirm the suspicion that the current system is flawed.

7. Even though the potential role of SES in the study was deemed to be minimal, it would still be worthwhile to continue to investigate the degree to which it is associated with student performance. Specifically, it might be

worthwhile to regress SES, board style, and performance indicators to see if or how they might be related.

8. In addition to examining the impact of SES, future research might also benefit from a look at a measure of community/ parent education as an independent variable. This may be a better measure of community support/interest in education than SES. Admittedly, this type of analysis may be difficult because the information may not be broken down by school district.

9. One final suggestion. If the data on per-pupil expenditures are available, it might be worthwhile to study the possible correlation or association of board style to expenditures. It is likely that professional boards may spend more because they may want to support quality education, and political boards may spend less because of taxpayer and parental pressures.

CHAPTER XVII

Indicators of School District Performance: Evidence of Student Achievement

Given that this study sought to determine the impact of school board policy-making styles on the educational performance of school districts, determining and operationalizing what constitutes good or poor performance is critically important.

In this section, a review of certain aspects or indicators of school district performance is presented. This includes a review of material in the education literature on what to look for in measuring the performance of school districts, and a review of how these variables are operationalized for testing purposes.

Any variable used in this study must ultimately relate to whether or how certain things that boards do at the governance level might manifest themselves at the district performance level. One might speculate, for instance, on how the act of hiring teachers on the basis of their being "hometown favorites" might affect the educational program of the district (Bryant & Grady, 1990). Or, in the example that Tallerico (1989) provided, one might wonder about the educational program of a district in which the school board neither respects nor accepts the superintendent's recommendation on educational matters and, instead, applies "a brake to administrative activities" (p. 26).

Support for using student achievement variables to compare the performance of school districts derives not only from the fact that it is contained in the education literature, but also because it is used by the New York State Education Department in its annual report card system. In the education literature as well, some researchers, including Allen (1996) and Gersie (1996), have used these student achievement indicators to measure the performance of schools and school districts. In a study of school effectiveness and achievement in Arkansas, for example, Allen (1996) utilized a set of indicators similar to those contained in the NYSED report card to determine if there are differences among school districts that have more or all effective schools and those that have fewer or no effective schools.

He surveyed 907 teachers from 54 different schools in 16 different districts who provided information about each district on the following set of indicators: dropout rate; attendance rate; completion rate; percentage of students achieving at or below the 25th, 50th, and 75th percentile on the state's (Arkansas Stanford Achievement) test; percentage of seniors who have taken the ACT; average ACT score; and percentage of students scoring at or above 19 on the ACT. The results revealed statistically significant differences in the performance ratings of the schools in the two school districts. The districts that have more or all effective schools received higher ratings than those that have fewer or no effective schools.

In this particular study, the specific tests and examinations used to measure the educational performance of school districts are as follows: (1) graduation and percent-to-college rates, (2) Pupil Evaluation Program, (3) Program Evaluation Tests, and (4) Regents Examinations. Each one of these subject areas is described below.

1. **Graduation and Percent to College Rates:**
   This set of student achievement indicators measures the following variables: (1) percent of Regents diplomas for 1988/89, (2) percent of Regents diplomas for 1996/97, and (3) percent of 1995/96 to college. The three indicators shown in Table 22-A below were excerpted from NYSED's *Statistical Profiles of Public School Districts*, 1998, p. vi.

Table 22-A
Student Performance Indicators—Graduation/College Attendance Rates

Study Variables	
1.	Percent of Regents diplomas for 1988/89
2.	Percent of Regents diplomas for 1996/97
3.	Percent of 1995/96 to college

SOURCE: *New York State Education Department (NYSED) 1998 Report to the Governor*

2. **Pupil Evaluation Program:**
   This component measures the percentage of students tested in Grade 3 Reading and Math, Grade 5 Writing, and Grade 6 Reading and Math that scored

above a minimum level of competence (the state reference point) and, therefore, were not identified as requiring remediation in 1996/97. The five indicators for the Pupil Evaluation Program are shown in Table 22-B below, which was excerpted from NYSED's *Statistical Profiles of Public School Districts*, 1998, p. ix. This type of testing has been in place for nearly 35 years at the elementary level and is principally the data source for placing schools under performance review.

Table 22-B
Student Performance Indicators—Pupil Evaluation Program

Study Variables	
1.	Grade 3 Reading
2.	Grade 3 Math
3.	Grade 5 Writing
4.	Grade 6 Reading
5.	Grade 6 Math

SOURCE: New York State Education Department (NYSED) 1998 Report to the Governor.

3. **Program Evaluation Tests**:
   This component measures student performance in each of the three parts of the grade 4 program evaluation test in science and for the total score on the grades 6 and 8 program evaluation tests in social studies in 1996/97. The Program Evaluation Test indicators listed below in Table 22-C were excerpted from NYSED's *Statistical Profiles of Public School*

Districts, 1998, p. ix. An important distinction between this and the PEP is that this test is used to evaluate instructional programs rather than to identify pupils in need of remediation.

Table 22-C
Student Performance Indicators—Program Evaluation Tests

Study Variables	
1.	Grade 4 Science, Objective Test (Content)
2.	Grade 4 Science, Objective Test (Skills)
3.	Grade 4 Science, Manipulative Skills
4.	Grade 6 Social Studies
5.	Grade 8 Social Studies

SOURCE: York State Education Department (NYSED) 1998 Report to the Governor.

4. **Regents Examinations:**
This component measures performance at the secondary level and has been in place now for more than 100 years. It contains information on the percent of average grades 9-12 enrollment tested, percent passing of the number tested, and the number passing as a percent of the average grade enrollment. This test was administered in January and June of the 1996/97 school year in the following subject areas: (1) Comprehensive English, (2) Global Studies, (3) U.S. History and Government, (4) Comprehensive French, (5) Comprehensive Spanish, (6) Sequential Mathematics Course I, (7) Sequential Mathematics

Course II, (8) Sequential Mathematics Course III, (9) Earth Science (1970 syllabus), (10) Biology, (11) Chemistry, and (12) Physics. The Regents indicators listed in Table 22-D below were excerpted from NYSED's *Statistical Profiles of Public School Districts*, 1998, p. ix.

Table 22-D

Student Performance Indicators—Regents Examinations Variables

Comprehensive English	1)	% of A.G.E. tested
	2)	% of tested passing
	3)	% of A.G.E. passing
Global Studies	4)	% of A.G.E. tested
	5)	% of tested passing
	6)	% of A.G.E. passing
U.S. History/Government	7)	% of A.G.E. tested
	8)	% of tested passing
	9)	% of A.G.E. passing
Comprehensive French	10)	% of A.G.E. tested
	11)	% of tested passing
	12)	% of A.G.E. passing
Comprehensive Spanish	13)	% of A.G.E. tested
	14)	% of tested passing
	15)	% of A.G.E. passing
Sequential Math 1	16)	% of A.G.E. tested
	17)	% of tested passing
	18)	% of A.G.E. passing
Sequential Math 2	19)	% of A.G.E. tested
	20)	% of tested passing
	21)	% of A.G.E. passing
Sequential Math 3	22)	% of A.G.E. tested
	23)	% of tested passing
	24)	% of A.G.E. passing
Earth Science-94 ED	25)	% of A.G.E. tested
	26)	% of tested passing
	27)	% of A.G.E. passing
Biology	28)	% of A.G.E. tested
	29)	% of tested passing
	30)	% of A.G.E. passing
Chemistry	31)	% of A.G.E. tested
	32)	% of tested passing
	33)	% of A.G.E. passing
Physics	34)	% of A.G.E. tested
	35)	% of tested passing
	36)	% of A.G.E. passing

SOURCE: *New York State Education Department (NYSED) 1998 Report to the Governor.* All of these indicators were adapted from the New York State Education Department

All of these indicators were adapted from NYSED's district performance assessment system, which is the *de facto* and *de jure* method of assessing the performance of school districts in the state. Assessing the validity or reliability of the report card system is beyond the scope of this study, although a report in the *Democrat and Chronicle* (Rosenberg & Whitmire, 1999) heralded New York's system as one of the best school accountability systems in the country. It should be noted, however, that the system does not rate every school nor does it provide rewards to the best performing schools as some states do. Nonetheless, it is the only system in place in New York State. Unless, and until, a good substitute is developed, the report card system will continue to be the official yardstick. The rationale in using these variables was that they help to capture variations in academic achievement outcomes among the two groups of school districts.

1. Summary

A review of the five studies on school board policy-making styles established the following key points. First, that there is a variety of school board policy-making styles that can be placed under two big umbrellas: professional (or right way) and political (or wrong way). Second, that those styles derive from certain overarching beliefs and/or educational philosophies on the part of the boards, be they expressed or implied. Third, that the board style and philosophy often translate into patterns of board actions or behaviors that ultimately impact district governance. Specific examples of some board member behaviors were also discussed in the context of educational governance. The impact of such behaviors on district governance, with a particular reference to superintendent tenure, was also discussed.

The section on district performance described the variables or indices that were used to determine what constitutes a good or poor educational performance. It also grouped and operationalized the performance categories as follows: (1) graduation rates/college rates, (2) Pupil Evaluation Program, (3) Program Evaluation Tests, and (4) Regents Examinations.

CHAPTER XVIII

A Review: New York State Education Law on Board-Superintendent Roles

In spite of what has been gleaned from the education literature on the need to clearly define and demarcate the roles of the board and superintendent, the education laws of New York State, Section 2554 of the New York State Education Law on the "Powers and Duties of the Board of Education" (see *McKinney's Consolidated Laws of New York Annotated*, Book 16, Section 2101-3200. p. 232) fall far short of providing clarity. This law outlines a wide-ranging set of roles and responsibilities for the board to the point of redundancy and confusion. Unlike the school board literature that ascribes policy making to the board and administration to the superintendent, the language of the New York State Education Law tends to give the two parties room to interpret or define their rights, roles, and responsibilities liberally; each party, therefore, interprets things in ways that serve their respective interests. A closer reading of this section of the law, however, reveals a hidden bias in favor of school boards in the sense that it grants boards more sweeping and overarching powers in district governance, especially in the area of personnel administration (Section 2554, Subdivision 2, p. 232). This has the effect of blurring the lines of role differentiation between the two parties and does more to weaken the superintendency.

A recent attempt to address the problems caused by the confusing language of the New York State Education Law was made by officials of the City of Rochester, New York, in 1994 during an education summit they convened to discuss the problem and attempt to find solutions. Specifically, city officials set out to determine, through a public process, the need for any legislative, regulatory, or management changes that may be necessary to improve performance within the district. Four major areas were examined: school district structure, governance, administrative and management, and regulation. Based on the overall public input, expert testimony, and staff analysis, the city administration identified three major goals on how to improve the district's performance. The primary goal of the city administration was to seek to "revise the State law to create a stronger Superintendent, with the Board of Education focusing on educational policy issues rather than personnel, finance, and other diverse concerns now forced on them by law."

The city subsequently identified sections of the New York State Education Law that address these areas (Sections 2554, 2566, 2556, and 2573) and sought legislative remedies in the New York state legislature. If this effort had been successful, it would have effectively strengthened or empowered the superintendency to allow for effective execution of district policies. This effort was also dubbed, "the strong superintendent form of district management" by officials in city government who played a leading and highly visible role in the education reform movement. In going through this summit, the city had hoped that it would force the Board of Education to focus on educational policy matters rather than on administrative minutia such as personnel administration.

By way of update, it should be noted that the efforts to strengthen the superintendency drew sharp criticism and opposition from the school board constituency, resulting in a compromise. On September 10, 1997, the New York State legislature amended Section 2554, Subdivision 2, and Section 2566, Subdivision 6 of the New York State Education Law, granting the superintendent only the power to appoint top aides in the district administration without the board's direction or approval. This was a far cry from the specific changes previously sought by the city administration and the superintendent.

The references made above to the confusion caused by the New York State Education Law warrants further comment. A more careful reading of this law revealed that there is not a uniform education law that applies to all districts in the state. Rather, what exists is volumes of legislation with numerous exceptions being granted to jurisdictions that have some political influence. This shotgun approach to legislating education hardly serves the institution well—it can only continue to add to the confusion as the continuing politicization of the educational process continues (Greene, 1992; Zeigler, Kehoe, & Reisman, 1985; Tucker & Zeigler, 1980). The Rochester situation is truly a case in point. If the New York State legislature deemed it important to grant the Rochester superintendent the power to appoint top aides, why might it not be worthwhile or warranted for the superintendents in other districts in that same state? Why was it not made a uniform ruling that all superintendents have the power to appoint top aids in their districts? Instead, such waivers would be granted on a case-by-case basis to selected jurisdictions.

Finally, the issue of how school board members enter into service is an equally important one to raise, especially as it relates to their conflicting roles and expectations. Tucker and Zeigler (1980) summed this up with their reference to the inherent "paradox" in the educational system (p. 2, 229). On the one hand, school districts are governmental units structured to operate as a democracy, complete with the election of board members, involvement of the public at board meetings, and so forth; while, at the same time, they call for "the growth of educational expertise" and for "school administrators to be professionals with degrees from recognized colleges of education" (p. 2). This inherent contradiction is a very important one relative to the role and expectations of, and by, school boards; it is also a contradiction that has been around since the inception of the district system 371 years ago (i.e., in 1642 in Boston, Massachusetts).

PART FOUR

References

ACT & Council for the Great City Schools (1991, January). Gateways to success: A report on urban student achievement and course-taking annual report.

Allen, R. W. (1996). *A comparison of school effectiveness and school achievement for schools in Arkansas*. (Unpublished doctoral dissertation). University of Arkansas, Arkansas.

Allison, D. (1996). *The clock starts ticking: The contract termination of four Alberta school superintendents* (Canada). (Unpublished doctoral dissertation). Arizona State University, Arizona.

Anderson, C. G. (1992). Behaviors of most effective and least effective school board members. *ERS Spectrum, 10*(3), 15-18.

Baker, D. (1997, June 15). The resurrection of 'the oldest textbook'; amid controversy, Christian Coalition pushes Bible history class in Florida public school district. *The Washington Post*, p. A3.

Banach, W. J. (1989). These eleven traits are the hallmarks of winning school board teams. *American School Board Journal, 176*(10), 23-24.

Blanchard, P. D. (1975). Small group analysis and the study of school board conflict: An interdisciplinary approach. *Small Group Behavior, 6*(2), 229-239.

Bolman, L. G., & Deal, T. E. (1991). *Reframing organizations: Artistry, choice, and leadership.* San Francisco, CA: Jossey-Bass Publishers.

Braddom, C. L. (1986). Prescription for improvement: Make certain your school board's system of evaluating the superintendent is fair, fast, factual, and frequent. *American School Board Journal, 173*(8), 28-29.

Bryant, M. T., & Grady, M. L. (1990). Where boards cross the line: Conflicts between boards and superintendents often revolve around questions of ethics. *American School Board Journal, 177*(10), 20-21.

Carpenter, D. A. (1989). Exemplary board members are made, not born, and here are the makings. *The American School Board Journal, 176*(10), 25-26.

Council for the Great City Schools (1999, February). Big-city students gain in reading achievement [Press release].

Council for the Great City Schools (1999, March). Council for the Great City Schools finds signs of progress in urban education: Urban school leaders voice greater optimism for future [Press release].

Czarnecki, E. H. (1996). *Factors influencing voluntary superintendent exiting in New York.* (Unpublished doctoral dissertation). State University of New York at Buffalo, Buffalo, New York.

Fink, A. (1991). *The survey handbook.* (Vol. 1). Thousand Oaks, CA: Sage Publications.

Gersie, M. F. (1996). *Increased expenditure and student achievement in selected New Jersey special needs districts.* (Unpublished doctoral dissertation). Wilmington College, Delaware.

Grady, M. L., & Bryant, M. T. (1991a). School board presidents tell why their superintendents fail. *Executive Educator, 13*(5), 24-25.

Grady, M. L., & Bryant, M. T. (1991b). School board turmoil and superintendent turnover: What pushes them to the brink? *School Administrator. 48*(2), 19-26.

Greene, K. R. (1990). School board members' responsiveness to constituents. *Urban Education, 24*(4), 363-375.

Greene, K. R. (1992). Models of school board policy-making. *Educational Administration Quarterly*, *28*(2), 220-236.

Haberman, M. (2003). Who benefits from failing urban school districts? The Haberman Educational Foundation, March

2003. Retrieved from: www.habermanfoundation.org/Articles/Default.aspx?id=06.

Hentges, J. T. (1986). The politics of superintendent-school board linkages: A study of power, participation, and control. *Spectrum*, *4*(3), 23-32.

Institute for Educational Leadership. (1986). School boards: Strengthening grass-roots leadership. Washington, DC: Author.

Janey, C. B. (1998, October). Superintendent's annual report [Annual Speech].

Katz, M. (1993). Matching school board and superintendent styles. *School Administrator*, *50*(2), 16-17, 19-20, 22-23.

Luehe, W. (1989). Fine-tuning keeps board/superintendent relations on track and running smoothly. *American School Board Journal*, *176*(10), 33, 42.

Lutz, F. W. (1980). Local school board decision making: A political-anthropological analysis. *Education and Urban Society*, *12*(4), 452-465.

Lutz, F. W., & Gresson, A. (1980). Local school boards as political councils. *Educational Studies*, *11*(2), 125-144.

Natale, J. (1990). School board ethics: On thin ice? *American School Board Journal*, *177*(10), 16-19.

National Commission on Excellence in Education. (1983). *A nation at risk: The imperative for educational reform.* Washington, DC: U.S. Government Printing Office.

New York State (1995). New York State Education Law. *McKinney's consolidated laws of New York Annotated.* Book 16, Section 2101-3200. Albany. St. Paul, MN: West Publishing Company.

New York State Education Department (NYSED). (February 1998a). New York: The state of learning: A report to the governor and the legislature on the educational status of the state's schools for 1997-98. Statewide Profile of the Educational System. Albany, NY: The State Education Department.

New York State Education Department (NYSED). (February 1996a). New York: The state of learning: A report to the governor and the legislature on the educational status of the state's schools for 1995-96. Statewide Profile of the Educational System. Albany, NY: The State Education Department.

New York State Education Department (NYSED). (February 1996b). New York: The state of learning: A report to the governor and the legislature on the educational status of the state's schools for 1995-96. Statistical Profiles of Public School Districts. Albany, NY: The State Education Department.

New York State Education Department (NYSED). (February 1996c). New York: The state of learning: A report to the governor and the legislature on the educational status of the state's schools for 1995-96. Computer Diskette on Statistical Profiles of Public School Districts. Albany, NY: The State Education Department.

Rada, R. D. (1988). A public choice theory of school board member behavior. *Educational Evaluation and Policy Analysis*, *10*(3), 225-236.

Rader, R., & McCarthy, P. (2011). School governance councils. *American School Board Journal*, November Edition. Retrieved from http://www.com/MainMenuCategory/Archive/2011/November/School-Governance-Councils.html.

Relic, P. D. (1986). Boards that try to administer school policy are courting complete chaos. *American School Board Journal*, *173* (9), 25-26.

Ritter, J. (1997, June). States stepping in at urban school in crisis. *USA Today*, p. A8.

Rosenberg, E., & Whitmire, R. (1999). Report on schools hails state. *Democrat and Chronicle*, p. 1B, Col. 2.

Ryan, T. P., Jr., Joiner, B. L., & Ryan, B. F. (1976). *Minitab student handbook*. North Scituate, MA: Duxbury Press.

Seaton, D. M., Underwood, K. E., & Fortune, J. C. (1992). The burden school board presidents bear. *American School Board Journal*, *179*(1), 32-37.

Shannon, T. A. (1989). What a superintendent can do about conflict with the school board. *American School Board Journal*, *176*(6), 25-27.

Simon, T. R. (Ed.). (1986). *Fundamentals of school board membership*. Trenton, NJ: School Boards Association.

Schaefer, R., & Farber, E. (1991). The student edition of MINITAB: Statistical software adapted for education. Addison-Wesley Publishing Company, Inc., & Benjamin/ Cummings Publishing Company, Inc.

Smith, R. W. (1986). Don't be snookered into handing your board's authority to the superintendent. *The American School Board Journal*, *173*(9), 23-24.

Spiropulos, G. G. (1996). *Superintendent turnover in Idaho, 1986-1994*. (Unpublished doctoral dissertation). University of Idaho, Idaho.

Steinberger, E. D. (1994). Superintendent-board relations that work. *The School Administrator*, *51*(7), 8-14.

Stone, D. A. (1988). *Policy paradox and political reason.* Cleveland, OH: Scott Foresman & Company.

Tallerico, M. (1989). What kind of a board member are you? Use these findings to size up your style. *American School Board Journal, 176*(10), 25-26.

Thurlow Brenner, C., Sullivan, G. L., & Dalton, E. (2002). Effective best practices for school boards: Linking local governance with student academic success. IPED Technical Reports. Paper 15. Retrieved from http://digitalcommons.utep.edu/iped_techrep/15.

Trotter, A., & Downey, G. W. (1989). Many superintendents privately contend school board "meddling" is more like it. *American School Board Journal, 176*(6), 21-25.

Tucker, H. J., & Zeigler, L. H. (1980). *Professionals versus the public: Attitudes, communication, and response in school districts*. New York, NY: Longman.

Weick, K. E. (June, 1982). Administering education in loosely coupled schools. *Phi Delta Kappan, 63*(10), 673-676.

Weil, N. C. (November, 1989). Public school reform dictates new responsibilities for school boards. *Journal of the New York State School Boards Association*, 20, 22-23, 31-32.

Weller, L. D., Brown, C. L., & Flynn, K. J. (1991). Superintendent turnover and school board member defeat. *Journal of Educational Administration, 29*(2), 61-71.

White House, Office of the Press Secretary. (May 19, 1999). Remarks by the president on education [Press release].

Zeigler, L. H. (1975). School board research: The problems and prospects. In P. J. Cistone (Ed.). *Understanding school boards*. Lexington, MA: D. C. Heath.

Zeigler, L. H., Kehoe, E., & Reisman, J. (1985). *City managers and school superintendents: Response to community conflict*. New York, NY: Praeger.

End Notes

End Notes

End Notes

End Notes

End Notes